George Eastman

George Eastman

BURNHAM HOLMES

Silver Burdett Press

For
Bill Stanton

CONSULTANTS:

Robert M. Goldberg
Consultant to the Social Studies
 Department
(formerly Department Chair)
Oceanside Middle School
Oceanside, New York

Kenneth H. Hilton
Social Studies Coordinator for the
 Rush-Henrietta Central Schools
Henrietta, New York

PHOTOGRAPH ACKNOWLEDGMENTS:
The Bettmann Archive: pp. 35, 80; Culver Pictures: p. 3; Reprinted courtesy Eastman
Kodak Company: pp. 5, 7, 9, 11, 29, 39, 50, 51, 62, 87, 97, 119, 127; International
Museum of Photography at George Eastman House: pp. 41, 79; UPI/Bettmann:
frontispiece.

AUTHOR'S ACKNOWLEDGMENTS:
I would like to thank the following for their assistance: Daphne Bartholomew at the
Poultney Public Library in Poultney, Vermont; Kathy Walkowicz, curator at the George
Eastman House in Rochester, New York; and Richard G. Gallin of Gallin House Press.

SERIES AND COVER DESIGN:
R STUDIO T Raúl Rodríguez and Rebecca Tachna

PHOTO RESEARCH:
Omni-Photo Communications, Inc.

Copyright © 1992 by Gallin House Press, Inc.

Published by Silver Burdett Press, Inc., a division of Simon & Schuster, Inc.,
250 James Street, Morristown, NJ 07960.

Library of Congress Cataloging-in-Publication Data

Holmes, Burnham.
George Eastman / Burnham Holmes.
p. cm.—(Pioneers in change)
Includes bibliographical references and index.
Summary: Describes the life of the man who revolutionized photography by
developing a camera simple enough for anyone to use.
1. Eastman, George, 1854–1932—Juvenile literature.
2. Photographic industry—United States—Biography—Juvenile literature.
[1. Eastman, George, 1854–1932. 2. Inventors. 3. Photography—History.]   I. Title.
II. Series.
TR140.E3H65   1991
338.7′61681418′092—dc20
[B]   91–10542
                                                              CIP
                                                               AC

Manufactured in the United States of America.
ISBN 0-382-24170-3   [lib. bdg.]
10 9 8 7 6 5 4 3 2 1
ISBN 0-382-24176-2 [pbk.]
10 9 8 7 6 5 4 3 2 1

CONTENTS

1

The Photographer as Magician

Taking a photograph nowadays is rarely the event it once was. At one time, though, the news of a photographer's arrival in town spread like wildfire. People would stop what they were doing, put on their finest clothes, and line up.

They came as family members, newlyweds, or one by one. Once inside the photographer's wagon turned into traveling studio, all watched in rapt attention as the photographer-magician prepared the magic box steadied on top of three wooden legs. (The front part of the magic box, or camera, contained the lens; the back part held the glass plate that was slid in at the last moment.) Then the mysterious figure disappeared beneath the black cloth.

"Hold it." The cap was removed from the end of the strange tube poking out from the camera.

1

Posing. Looking at the magic box, at the strange eye tube. Sitting perfectly still, wondering: *Do I feel any different? Does it matter what I'm thinking about? Will my thoughts show up, too?*

"Just a little longer. You're doing fine."

What will I look like? Will I look like myself? How much longer is this going to take?

"Okay." The cap went back on the tube. "That's all. You can relax now. I'll have your picture ready in a jiffy... er, in a few minutes anyway."

"Ah, excuse me. Would it be all right if I watched?"

The magician-photographer drew back a small overhead curtain. A yellow pane of glass filtered the light in from outdoors. Then this mysterious person walked over to a sink to pour a mixture from a bottle over the plate. Magically, in a minute or so, the dark outline of a person began to appear on the white background of the glass plate.

The photographer-magician dipped the plate into a pan of liquid for a few seconds and lifted it up to drip-dry. Next, the plate was washed with water, drip-dried, and placed in a frame.

Then, in the natural light of day, the magician-photographer held out the developed picture. Enclosed in a decorative frame, it was the spitting image of the sitter. In the words of a writer and doctor from Boston, Oliver Wendell Holmes, it was "a mirror with a memory."

"So that's what I look like to others. Well, I'll be a monkey's uncle."

For many, a picture tucked into an inexpensive tin frame or a more expensive leather-bound box lined with plush and fastened with a gold- or silver-colored hook, was

A portrait camera of the 1860s. A metal gadget (on the left) was used to hold still the head of the person being photographed.

a once-in-a-lifetime chance to capture and hang onto their likeness. Such a photograph often became one of their most treasured possessions.

Today, when people look at these old portraits, they are often struck by how stiff and uncomfortable those in the photographs look. It was not only because their suits may have been scratchy or their dresses too warm for the day; rather it was because these people gazing out at you from the past had to remain still for a long time. To help people maintain their poses, photographers often used a metal gadget shaped like a half moon on the end of an iron rod to hold the head motionless. It's no wonder that people look so rigid and unnatural in these old photographs.

Besides the unnaturalness of the poses, the viewer may find it strange looking at these old photographs because she or he is participating in the history of something that happened a long time ago. The critic and philosopher Roland Barthes discussed this aspect in his book *Camera Lucida*.

> One day, quite some time ago, I happened on a photograph of Napoleon's youngest brother, Jerome, taken in 1852. And I realized then, with an amazement I have not been able to lessen since: "I am looking at eyes that looked at the Emperor."

In 1857, when he was only three years old, George Eastman sat still for a photographer traveling through his hometown in upstate New York. His portrait serves as a record of Eastman's earliest contact with photography.

Three-year-old George Eastman.

2

George Eastman's Brief Childhood

George Eastman, the youngest of three children, was born on July 12, 1854. In that year, there were thirty-one stars sewn on the American flag. Franklin Pierce was president. Only about 25 million people lived in the United States.

George had two sisters. Emma Kate was four years older than George. Ellen Maria, who was eight years older, was already helping out with chores around the house. These three children lived with their mother, Maria Kilbourn Eastman, and their father, George Washington Eastman, in Waterville, a small town in upstate New York. (In the 1600s, ancestors of the Eastmans and the Kilbourns had moved from England to North America.)

In 1842, George Washington Eastman had founded Eastman's Commercial College. Located seventy miles

George Eastman's father, George Washington Eastman, founded a business school in Rochester, New York.

away in Rochester, New York, this school was on the fourth floor of the most important building in the city.

Eastman's Commercial College specialized in training people in double-entry bookkeeping (a complete record showing both the money going out and the money coming in for every business dealing), penmanship, and even spelling. Courses ran from four to eight weeks.

Eastman's Commercial College tried to teach other things as well, as can be glimpsed in the following rhyme from a textbook on penmanship coauthored by George W. Eastman:

> My boy, be cool,
> Do things by rule,
> And then you'll do them right....

Overseeing the teachers and students and ensuring that the school ran smoothly took up most of Eastman's time. Consequently, the Eastman children didn't see their father nearly as often as they would have liked. Whenever he returned to Waterville, it was a special occasion.

Young George grew up filled with wonder and curiosity, not to mention questions. When he visited his father's nearby greenhouse, for instance, young George might ask so many questions that the men who worked for his father's plant nursery would be hard pressed to get any work done pruning fruit trees for sale or transplanting Maria Eastman's prize flowers.

It seemed as if George was always trying to figure out how things worked. As he grew older, George would remain just as curious. As an adult George Eastman would still try to understand the principles behind how things worked.

In 1860, the Eastman family moved to Rochester. George and his sisters could now see their father more often. They would even be able to go down to the railway station as a family to see and hear the newly elected president, Abraham Lincoln, as he whistle-stopped his way from Illinois to Washington, D.C.

Rochester was not only a city that offered new sights and sounds, but it was also home to many important people. Frederick Douglass, the African-American writer

George Eastman's mother, Maria Kilbourn Eastman.

and editor, lived in Rochester. Douglass had spent the first twenty years of his life as a slave. Later, he became one of the most stirring speakers in the United States and a leader to the abolitionists, those who wanted to abolish slavery. Rochester was also the home of Susan B. Anthony, a leader of the antislavery movement. In later years, Anthony would be a leading suffragist, advocating the extension of the right to vote, especially for women.

But almost as quickly as things had taken a turn for the better for the Eastman family, life made a tragic about-face. On April 27, 1862, George Washington Eastman unexpectedly died. It came as a total shock to the family. Eastman hadn't even been ill. At the time, young George was only seven years old.

Eastman was sorely missed by his family. In addition to their grief, the Eastman family always seemed to be in need of money. Maria Eastman took in lodgers in an attempt to make ends meet. Nevertheless, the money pressures continued to mount.

George Eastman's world had turned upside down. He had to grow up quickly after the death of his father. At first, George thought he could earn money by making and selling wood shelves. But after lots of work, he earned only five dollars selling his shelves. Understandably, George didn't see much point in continuing this project.

George longed to make a sizable contribution to the family finances, to step into his father's shoes. In addition to the mounting financial problems, Emma Kate was crippled with polio and had to walk with crutches. The youngest Eastman decided that what he really needed to do was to go out and get a real job. Going to school was beginning to seem less and less important in George's eyes than working and bringing home a regular salary.

A family friend, Captain Cornelius Waydell, offered George a job at his insurance company. For serving as a messenger boy, George would be paid three dollars a week. He would be on the run from morning to night, warned Captain Waydell. But George was never one to shy away from hard work and a challenge.

George Eastman at age thirteen, five years after his father's death.

Maria Eastman was reluctant to let George drop out of school. Nevertheless, George insisted. If he could get a job, George told his mother, he would be able to help out with the ever-growing household bills that had to be paid. Besides, then he would always have enough money to buy a book on any subject that interested him.

On March 8, 1868, only four months shy of his fourteenth birthday, George quit public school and went to work. This was the end of his formal education. By no means, however, did it signal a stop to George Eastman's longing for learning and improvement both for himself and others.

What sort of a prospective employee did Captain Waydell see standing before him? George was a thin teenager of medium height with dark hair and blue-gray eyes. He appeared naturally shy, which some might have called good manners. Though he only spoke when spoken to, George was also bright and eager. When he did talk, he always seemed to have something worthwhile to say. Otherwise, he remained quiet.

That first year, George worked his way up from messenger and office boy to clerk. After paying a few bills at home, he cleared thirty-nine dollars. With some of the extra money, George bought some photographs and frames. This was the first indication that George had an interest in photography. But even in the beginning, George always put away some of his money. In later years, he explained his attitude toward saving in this way: "I was brought up to fear debt, and as a matter of fact in the early years I always saved something every year no matter what my salary was."

The next year, George began work for another insurance company for a salary of thirty-five dollars a month.

Over the next couple of years, George was given more responsibilities and salary. Not only was he able to give more money to his mother for the upkeep of the house, but he was also able to buy more tools. Along with his curiosity about how things worked, George was developing a real skill at working with his hands.

In April 1874, at the age of nineteen, George left the insurance company to work as a junior bookkeeper at the Rochester Savings Bank. Within two years, he was making $1,400 a year. (Fourteen hundred dollars would equal approximately $15,400 in 1992 dollars.) George would certainly have made his business-school father proud.

It was about this time that George bought a flute on the installment plan. His payments for the flute, however, turned out to be more successful than his flute playing. Two years later, Eastman's rendition of the song "Annie Laurie" was barely recognizable.

Although George Eastman showed promise, a career in insurance or banking didn't really interest him. Eastman's thoughts were speeding off in a very different direction.

Around Thanksgiving 1877, when Eastman was twenty-three, he withdrew money from his savings account and bought close to $100 worth of photography equipment. At the same time, he signed up for photography lessons with George H. Monroe, a local photographer.

Eventually Eastman became more interested in the practical side of photography than in the artistic side. How cameras and glass plates worked, how he could make them work better—those were the things that especially intrigued him. Although photography may have begun only as a hobby, it was not to remain one for long. Photography was soon to become George Eastman's passion.

3

The Origins of Photography

The world of photography that George Eastman had recently entered had been around for a long time. The earliest known camera was called a *camera obscura*. These two Latin words mean "dark room." Aristotle, the famous Greek philosopher, developed the idea over 2,300 years ago in his observations of the eclipse of the sun. Over 1,200 years ago, an Arabian astronomer and optician named Alhazen used a camera obscura and spoke of it in these words:

> If the image of the sun at the time of an eclipse—provided it is not a total one—passes through a small round hole on to a plane surface opposite, it will be crescent-shaped.... The image of the sun only shows this property when the hole is very small.

During the 1400s the camera obscura found wide use, primarily in helping artists sketch from nature. The Italian artist and engineer Leonardo da Vinci observed one and entered the following description in a notebook:

When the images of illuminated objects pass through a small round hole into a very dark room, if you receive them on a piece of white paper placed vertically in the room at some distance from the aperture (the small round hole or opening), you will see on the paper all those objects in their natural shapes and colours. They will be reduced in size, and upside down, owing to the intersection of the rays at the aperture.

(You can observe the workings of the camera obscura by using a table lamp, a magnifying glass, and a sheet of white paper. Turn on the light of the table lamp, hold the magnifying glass in one hand about two feet away from the lamp, and in the other hand hold the paper about one foot beyond the magnifying glass. Adjust these distances until you are able to see clearly the upside-down image of the table lamp on the piece of paper.)

If the camera obscura could display the image, what could be used to make the image permanent? In 1725, Johann Heinrich Schultze, a professor of science at a German university, mixed chalk, silver, and nitric acid in a flask. The mixture became silver nitrate. When the flask was held up to the sunlight, the silver nitrate changed from white to purple.

Later, Schultze cut out letters from a piece of paper and wrapped the paper around the flask. "Before long," observed Schultze, "I found out that the sun's rays on the side on which they had touched the glass through the apertures [holes] in the paper, wrote the words or the sentences so accurately and distinctly on the chalk sediment, that many people...were led to attribute the result to all kinds of artifices [trickery]."

Schultze was one of the first people to apply chemistry to what would soon become the field of photography. The chemicals that would later most often be used in photography are the silver halides, especially silver iodide, silver chloride, and silver bromide.

Thomas Wedgwood's father, Josiah Wedgwood, was a potter who developed the process for making Wedgwood pottery that is still popular today. His factories produced many new kinds of pottery and ceramics. His son Thomas, however, struck out on his own. Thomas Wedgwood experimented with recording an image on paper that had been coated with silver nitrate, one of the most important chemicals in photography.

In 1802, Thomas Wedgwood published an article on his findings. It contained the following passage:

White paper, or white leather, moistened with solution of nitrate of silver, undergoes no change when kept in a dark place; but, on being exposed to the day light, it speedily changes colour, and, after passing through different shades of grey and brown, becomes at length nearly black.

The full title of this article was "An Account of a Method of Copying Paintings upon Glass and of Making Profiles by the Agency of Light upon Nitrate of Silver, with Observations by H. Davy." Sir Humphry Davy was a leading English chemist at that time. Wedgwood and Davy called the profiles discussed in their article "shadowgraphs" or "photograms."

The major drawback of these images was stated by Sir Humphry Davy himself: "Nothing but a method of preventing the unshaded parts of the delineation [picture] from being coloured by exposure to the day is wanting, to render the process as useful as it is elegant." In other words, Wedgwood and Davy needed a fixer, a chemical to stop the picture from turning totally black.

The long title of Wedgwood and Davy's article brings into focus two of the driving forces behind the development of photography. One was the frustration of certain artists. Looking at the image projected by the camera obscura, artists wished they could draw or paint better in order to copy what they saw. A few of these people were moved to do something to overcome their shortcomings. Instead of using pens and brushes to transfer the scene, they worked to find a way to record the image directly onto paper.

A second force behind the development of photography was that for centuries only rich people could afford to have their portraits painted. Many of these portraits hang in art museums around the world. During the Renaissance, Giorgio Vasari wrote about Titian, the greatest painter of Venice: "There was almost no lord, nor prince, nor great lady, who was not painted by Titian." With the rise of the middle class during the nineteenth century, however, more and more people wanted to own a permanent record of how they looked. Some had miniature portraits painted, but even these were too expensive for most people. A demand existed for an inexpensive way to record a person's likeness.

Paper silhouettes quickly filled this need and soon

became popular. They could be done simply enough, only requiring a pair of scissors, a strong light, and black paper. A silhouette, or outline, usually showed the shape of a person's head—often cut out from black paper—but it certainly did not include very many of the details that go into making an individual unique. Also, the quality of the silhouette totally depended upon the skill of the artist. A way was still needed to capture and make a permanent copy of everything that could be seen through a camera obscura.

Thomas Wedgwood had been unsuccessful in his attempts to fix the image. "The images formed by means of a camera obscura, have been found to be too faint to produce, in any moderate time, an effect upon the nitrate of silver," he wrote.

The honor of making the first photograph fell to Joseph Nicéphore Niepce, a French physicist with a special interest in lithography (the art of printing from a flat surface, such as stone, that has been drawn on with a grease crayon). Niepce did not work with paper sensitized with silver nitrate. Instead, he tried using a camera obscura that cast its upside-down image onto a pewter plate coated with a special substance called bitumen of Judea.

The year was 1826. Niepce pointed a camera obscura out of a second-story window of his house in Saint-Loup-de-Varennes in southern France. For eight hours he exposed a pewter plate to the view outside his workroom window. Afterward, he washed the plate with a mixture of lavender oil and white petroleum, or turpentine. The bitumen of Judea on some areas of this plate had been affected by the light and had grown hard, producing light areas. The bitumen on other parts of the plate had washed off, leaving dark areas of pewter.

Although *View from a Window at Gras* has the distinction of being the world's oldest photograph, Niepce's sun picture, or *heliograph* ("written with light"), may strike today's observer as looking more like an abstract painting. On closer examination, though, one is able to make out—from left to right—a pigeon house, a tree, a barn roof, and part of Niepce's house. Oddly enough, the sunlight is streaming toward both the left and right sides of the picture. That's because the earth rotated during the long time it took to expose or subject the pewter plate to light.

One of the first eyewitnesses to the beginnings of photography was Philip Hone, an American in Paris. "I went this morning...to see a collection of the views made by the wonderful process lately discovered in France by Monsieur Daguerre, which is called by his name," he wrote.

This new milestone in photography was made in 1839 by the Frenchman Louis Jacques Mandé Daguerre. For years, people had entered Daguerre's theater in Paris to see his paintings—perhaps a majestic cathedral in England or the peaceful countryside of Switzerland—projected into seventy-foot-high pictures. As the creator of these lifelike scenes in his diorama, Daguerre had long been using the camera obscura. This is what had eventually led Daguerre along the road to photography and to the exhibition of daguerreotypes that Hone wrote about in his diary.

"The pictures he has are extremely beautiful—they consist of views in Paris, and exquisite collections of objects of still life," continued Hone.

The manner of producing them constitutes one of the wonders of modern times, and, like other miracles, one may almost be excused for disbelieving it without seeing the very process by which it is created. Every object, however minute, is a perfect transcript [copy] of the thing itself; the hair of the human head, the gravel on a roadside, the texture of a silk curtain, or the shadow of the smaller leaf reflected upon the wall, are all imprinted as carefully as nature or art has created them in the objects transferred....

To create "one of the wonders of modern times" Daguerre used a copper plate, first covered with silver and then polished. The plate was then washed, coated with iodine vapor (that turned into silver iodide), and placed in a camera obscura. This treated plate made possible camera exposures of less time. (Still, the exposures took so long that many of the street scenes were without pedestrians and horse-drawn carriages. Why? Because in order to appear in the daguerreotype, everything needed to remain motionless. By the time the scene had been daguerreotyped, the horses had trotted and the people had walked right out of the picture.) After the plate had been exposed, it was then held over a dish of heated mercury. The mercury vapor brought out the light areas of the scene. The polished silver retained the dark areas.

A way to speed up the time necessary to make a daguerreotype was needed. Josef Petzval, a professor of mathematics at the University of Vienna, advanced the state of photography when he added a better lens to the camera used for making daguerreotypes. (A lens is a piece of glass—or nowadays often plastic—that focuses the light to form an image.) There were four glass parts to Petzval's lens. The wider aperture, or opening, allowed sixteen times more light to enter the camera, and the lens was thirty times faster than other lenses. (The speed of a lens is how long it takes to expose a picture; a fast lens takes less time.) Consequently, the exposure time was speeded up from many hours to a matter of minutes.

Petzval's lens gave the daguerreotype a sharp, clear image and made it the most popular portrait lens for the next fifty years. Even today, there are still some daguerreotypes in fine condition, especially those that were treated with gold. This seems even more remarkable when contrasted with the modern photographs in family albums that are already beginning to fade.

As good as the daguerreotype might have been, however, it did not lead to further breakthroughs in photography. Why? Because the process proved too slow and expensive. Consequently, most interest in the daguerreotype began to disappear after only twenty years.

For the new direction that photography would take, the scene shifted to the English inventor William Henry Fox Talbot. While on a trip to Italy in 1833, Talbot was thinking over his past experience with the camera obscura. He wrote:

> And this led me to reflect on the inimitable [unable to be imitated or matched] beauty of the pictures of nature's painting which the glass lens of the Camera throws upon the paper in its focus—fairy pictures, creatures of a moment, and destined as rapidly to fade away.
>
> It was during these thoughts that the idea occurred to me...how charming it would be if it were possible to cause these natural images to imprint themselves durably, and remain fixed upon the paper! ...And since, according to chemical writers, the nitrate of silver is a substance peculiarly sensitive to the

action of light, I resolved to make a trial of it, in the first instance, whenever occasion permitted on my return to England.

Later he would have that chance. In 1835 Talbot took pictures of buildings using a camera obscura. By alternating washes of salt and silver, and keeping the film moist, he reduced the time it took to make a clear image to only ten minutes.

Talbot was basically doing what Wedgwood had done. "It is curious and interesting and certainly establishes their claim as the inventors of the photographic art," observed Talbot about the findings of Wedgwood and Davy. "[T]hough the actual progress they made in it was small."

When Talbot put together a collection of his pictures in one of the first photography publications, he described them by the title of a "Process by which Natural Objects May be Made to Delineate Themselves without the Aid of the Artist's Pencil." Talbot had succeeded in overcoming his shortcomings as an artist.

Over the next few years Talbot put together many cameras of lenses on wooden boxes (his wife referred to them as mousetraps) and experimented with silver iodide on paper brushed with gallo-nitrate of silver—a combination of silver, acetic acid, gallic acid, and water. What Talbot eventually achieved was a negative-positive process.

The negative was what the camera had recorded, and it showed the light values reversed. The dark areas of the negative were the light areas of the scene and picture; the light areas of the negative were the darker areas of the picture. In order to change the negative to the way the scene had originally appeared, the negative had to be printed. The print of the negative would then be the positive. In 1839 Talbot invented and described this "photographic drawing."

Talbot's process was unlike all previous photographic experiments. With the daguerreotype, the picture had been one of a kind. If another copy were desired, the daguerreotype would have to be daguerreotyped. Talbot's advance allowed any number of pictures to be made from a single negative.

An equally important contribution was the English astronomer Sir John Frederick William Herschel's use of sodium thiosulfate as a fixing agent. Known to this day as hypo (because it was mistakenly thought to be sodium hyposulfite), this fixer stopped the film from any further development by removing the excess silver salts.

By 1841 Talbot had perfected his method and taken out a patent. To take out a patent means to register an idea and design with the government. A patent is a government document giving the inventor rights to the invention for a limited time. A patent gives the inventor the right to prevent others from making, using, or selling the invention. Talbot's process, known as the calotype (meaning "beautiful picture") process, gave rise to modern photography.

There were problems, though, with the calotype. It was hard to get a sharp, detailed print from the paper negative. Also, the prints tended to fade after a short time. So, the search continued to discover a better way to record the camera's image.

"I yesterday succeeded in producing a photograph *on glass* having very much the character of his [Daguerre's] results," wrote Herschel in a letter to Talbot in 1839.

Herschel's method was to deposit a film of muriate of

silver, or silver chloride, on the glass. After drying and then washing it with nitrate, he focused the camera on the sensitized side of the glass. The results were better than with paper.

In 1851, twelve years after Talbot had first invented his photographic process, Frederick Scott Archer, an English sculptor and photographer, wrote about his experiments with collodion [pronounced kuh-LOHD-ee-uhn], a type of guncotton (a highly explosive nitrate, or salt, of nitric acid) soaked in ether. Archer's goal was to take photographs of the people who modeled for him so that he could use these studies for his sculptures.

First, Archer cleaned a glass negative. Then he poured a combination of collodion mixed with potassium iodide. Soon the surface of the glass became sticky. (Collodion comes from a Greek word meaning "to adhere" or "stick to.") While the plate was still wet, it was loaded into the camera. Usually, the camera was already mounted on the tripod, a three-legged stand, and focused on the scene to be photographed. After exposure, the plate was immediately developed.

The advantage of Archer's wet-collodion process over the calotype process was that the image that it produced was sharper. The advantage of Archer's process over the daguerreotype process was that the exposure required only a few seconds.

A variation of the wet-collodion process was used to produce the ambrotype. An ambrotype was produced by exposing a glass negative, bleaching it, and placing a black background against the positive on the glass. This process was similar to the daguerreotype process in that it produced only one picture; there was no negative from which later copies could be made. A cheaper variation of the ambrotype was the ferrotype, or tintype. The name came from using a thin sheet of darkened metal to make the positive.

The wet-collodion process would change the way people looked at the American Civil War. This would be a war that was not only read about or talked about. Photographs were actually taken on the scene.

The combination of sharper image and shorter exposure time of the wet-collodion process would allow the American photographer Mathew Brady and his team of nineteen adventuresome fellow photographers, most notably Alexander Gardner, to record what they saw in great detail.

The disadvantages of the wet-collodion process were that for each picture the photographer had to treat the glass plate with chemicals, use the plate while it was still wet, and develop the plate immediately after he or she took the picture. For if the wet plate was not used within about ten minutes after preparation, it began to lose its sensitivity.

Even in the studio, all the equipment needed in the wet-collodion process wasn't always easy to keep track of. But to use this process outdoors, the photographer had to carry a supply of glass plates, chemicals, pans, pure water, a darkroom, a tripod for holding the camera steady, and, of course, a camera.

During the Civil War the photographer's wagon, creaking under the heavy load of photographic supplies, was often spotted by soldiers who greeted it by its nickname of "Whatsit" ("What is it?"). But all the equipment that Brady and the others needed for the wet-collodion process made it possible even for people far away from the front lines to feel the immediate impact of what it was like to be in that war. Brady was on target when he declared that "the camera is the eye of history."

Wet-collodion photography was what the young George Eastman would learn when he first became interested in photography.

4

A Portrait of Eastman as a Young Businessman

George Eastman paid five dollars to George H. Monroe for lessons in how to carry out the wet-collodion process. This was the system of plunging a clean glass plate into a solution of guncotton and ether in order to create a sticky surface on the glass. After that, the plate was dipped into silver nitrate. The glass plate was then slid into the holder at the back of the camera. The photograph was finally ready to be taken.

After the exposure of the glass negative, the plate needed to be developed immediately. The photographer went into a dark tent and poured solutions over the glass. This prepared the plate for printing. Then, after the photographer pressed paper to the glass and exposed it to light, the image would be transferred from the glass plate onto the paper.

The word *photography*, coined by Sir John Herschell in 1839, comes from Greek and means "light writing." The word was probably a combination of Talbot's *photo*genic (which means "produced by light") and Niepce's helio-*graph*. In any case, there was nothing light about the photo-graphic equipment that Eastman hauled around with him.

Later, George Eastman recalled his early experience in photography:

[I]n those days, one did not take a camera, one accompanied the outfit of which the camera was only a part. I bought an outfit and learned that it took not only a strong but also a dauntless [fearless] man to be an outdoor photographer.

My layout [outfit], which included only the essentials, and in it a camera about the size of a soap box [a large box or case for packing and shipping soap], a tripod which was strong and heavy enough to support a bungalow [small house], a big plate-holder, a dark-tent, a nitrate bath, and a container for water. The glass plates were not, as now, in the holder ready for use; they were what is known as "wet plates"—that is, glass which had to be coated with collodion and then sensitized with nitrate of silver in the field just before exposure. Hence the nitrate of silver was something that always had to go along and it was perhaps the most awkward companion imaginable on a journey. Being corrosive [destructive; able to wear metal away slowly by chemical action], the container had to be of glass and the cover tight—for silver nitrate is not a liquid to get intimate with. The first time that I took a silver bath away with me, I wrapped it with exceeding great care and put it in my trunk. The cover leaked, the nitrate got out, and stained most of my clothing.

This 1877 view of Rochester, New York, is George Eastman's first photograph.

But neither the expense, the weight of the equipment, nor the difficulty of making photographs discouraged Eastman. He wrote:

Being an amateur was, I suppose, arduous work, but one never finds a hobby hard riding and I went out taking photographs whenever I could, read everything that was written on the subject, and generally tried to put myself on the plane of the professional photographer without, however, any idea of going into the business of photography. Since I took my views mostly outdoors—I had no studio—the bulk of the paraphernalia [equipment] worried me. It seemed that one ought to be able to carry less than a pack-horse load.

His experiences may not have discouraged George Eastman, but they did make him very aware of many of the problems in photography that begged to be solved.

The first difficulty that Eastman set out to tackle was the problem of the photographic plates. He read widely in the field of photography. He was even studying French and German so that he could learn about advances in photography printed in those languages. Reading through the *British Journal of Photography* one day, Eastman ran across an article that sparked his interest: "The English article started me in the right direction. I began in my spare time—for I was still working in the bank—to compose an emulsion [mixture] that could be coated and dried on the glass plate and retain its properties long enough to be used in the field and thus avoid lugging around the dark-tent [a portable darkroom] and silver bath."

With all the difficulties—the weight and amount of

equipment and the steps necessary for processing a single exposure—a full day of photographing in the field often resulted in only six photographs.

"My first results did not amount to much," admitted Eastman, "but finally I came upon a coating of gelatine [gelatin: a gluelike material obtained from animal skin, bones, and hair by boiling] and silver bromide that had all the necessary photographic qualities.... At first I wanted to make photography simpler merely for my own convenience, but soon I thought of the possibilities of commercial production." His "dry plates" were much more convenient to use than the "wet plates."

Eastman's shift from a strictly personal interest in photography to an interest in the wider applications of photography was something that would affect people everywhere. George Eastman never seemed to get involved in anything only halfway. If anything, once involved in a project he would work twice as hard.

For Eastman, it was as if each day were actually divided into two days. The first day was spent at his job in the bank. He worked hard and was considered to have a bright future there. His second workday began after he arrived home. After dinner, Eastman would set up all his equipment in the kitchen and carry out photographic experiments long into the night. "I retained my place in the Savings Bank until Sept. 1881," recalled Eastman later, "giving the business [of working on photography] what attention I could between the hours of three P.M. [when the bank closed] and breakfast time."

Maria Eastman worried about her son's health. She would remind him that he always looked tired. He was losing weight. He wasn't getting enough exercise. However, she did have to admit that he seemed happier.

The relationship between Maria and George Eastman was a close one. Over a span of fifty-three years they shared the same home—first in the one-and-a-half-story frame house in Waterville, then in three houses in Rochester: the house that George W. Eastman had bought, the three-story house that George Eastman bought in 1890, and later the thirty-seven-room Georgian-style mansion that George Eastman built in 1905.

By June 1879, Eastman had not only developed a good emulsion for coating glass plates but had also developed a machine for applying it. He would now be able to coat the glass plates faster as well as evenly. Uniformity, staying close to a high standard, would become the hallmark of George Eastman's photographic products.

Withdrawing $400 from his savings, Eastman traveled to London, the photographic capital of the world. Eastman may have heard about the life of Frederick Scott Archer, the Englishman who had developed the wet-collodion process. Although Archer had been responsible for making modern photography possible, he unfortunately had not taken out a patent on his wet-collodion process. In 1857, Archer had died at the age of forty-four, a broken and penniless man.

In any case, Eastman was determined that nothing like that would ever happen to him. Eastman would always protect himself with patents. On July 22, 1879, Eastman received his British patent. While in London, he also granted two companies the license to use his invention. Soon after, he was on board a ship for the return voyage to New York City. George was eager to get home to Rochester, for there was so much work to do.

"In the preparation of gelatine dry-plates, great difficulty has heretofore been encountered in spreading the gelatine emulsion evenly over the glass," read the application for a U.S. patent submitted in September 1879. "By my improved process plates are covered with a perfectly uniform coating of gelatine emulsion, extending entirely out to the edges of the plates, and this result is accomplished very much more rapidly than inferior plates are produced by the old method."

As usual, George Eastman was thinking far ahead. "I am as yet connected with photography as an amateur only but am making preparations to engage in the manufacture of Gelatin Plates on a *large scale* and expect my invention to enable me, if necessary, to *put* the *price down*." By the next April, Eastman held patents for his invention from both the United States and Great Britain.

The next major step for the ambitious Eastman was to rent the third-floor loft of a large factory building in downtown Rochester. There he worked to perfect an improved machine to coat the plates. By Thanksgiving 1880, three years after George Eastman had first started out in photography, he was set to launch his own business.

Two of Maria Eastman's lodgers were Colonel and Mrs. Henry Alvah Strong. The colonel, a partner in a buggy-whip company, was the type of person who was always on the lookout for new business opportunities. As he listened to the studious-looking young man, the colonel grew excited. Convinced of the soundness of Eastman's ideas, the colonel invested $1,000. And on January 1, 1881, the Eastman Dry Plate Company was officially incorporated, that is, legally formed into a corporation or organization of employers and employees.

Word about the quality and dependability of Eastman's dry plates quickly spread among photographers. Attracted by the possibilities of Eastman's dry plates was E.

& H. T. Anthony Company of New York City. The Anthony Company, the largest photographic supply house in the country, wanted the exclusive rights to sell Eastman's dry plates.

Before long, Eastman was shipping $4,000 worth of dry plates every month. Eastman was so encouraged by the large volume of business that in September 1881 he quit his job at the bank. He was now free to devote his full attention to the business of photography. The Eastman Dry Plate Company had become an official part of the business landscape of Rochester.

One photographer who said he would "use nothing else" but Eastman's Gelatine Dry Plates was William Kurtz, a photographer famous for his cabinet cards.

What were cabinet cards? These were photographs mounted on heavy 4 x 5½-inch paper cards that were then popular among collectors. There were even special albums to put cabinet cards in. A person, of course, could have a cabinet card made of himself or herself. But more often, people bought cabinet cards already made. Printed by the thousands, these cards were usually of famous people, such as actors, actresses, artists, politicians, singers, writers, even members of the British royal family. Wildly popular and widely available, cabinet cards were like today's baseball cards.

The public was also hungry for photographs of natural landmarks, such as Niagara Falls and the Grand Canyon. These were especially popular when accompanied by a lifelike appearance of depth.

To produce a feeling of depth, the photographer used a binocular, or twin-lens, camera to record two close but slightly different photos of the same scene. These photos were then printed side by side on a strip of cardboard that

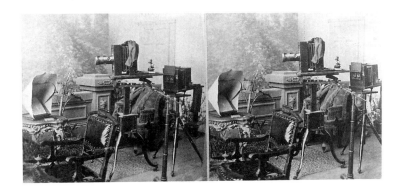

This is a stereoscopic card showing two slightly different pictures of a photographer's studio. The taller camera is a portrait camera, and the one with two lenses is a stereo camera.

felt and looked like a heavy postcard. The photos were then placed in a special viewer called a stereoscope.

The American writer and doctor Oliver Wendell Holmes had designed the stereoscope used in the United States. At one end was the card holder, and at the other end were the lenses. The lenses could be slid toward or away from the card in order to correct the focus. Holding the stereoscope by the handle underneath and pointing it toward a light, the observer would peer through the lenses at one end toward the photos at the other end. The two photographs would seem to merge into one three-dimensional picture. (Although Holmes had invented the model that became popular, he did not patent it. For that reason, he did not receive a penny for his idea.)

After all the excitement of Eastman's early success, disaster suddenly struck. Photographers began to complain that Eastman Gelatine Dry Plates were no longer any good. The plates had lost their sensitivity.

Eastman investigated and discovered that the Anthony Company had been selling only the fresh dry plates as they arrived. However, with the increase in demand, they had begun to sell old plates stacked in the storeroom. Eastman had found out the hard way that glass plates lost their sensitivity with age.

Eastman made it a point to refund all the money for the bad plates. This plunged him into debt, but George Eastman wanted to build a feeling of trust in what he sold.

An even more serious problem surfaced as he began to make additional plates. The old formula that he had developed no longer seemed to work. Eastman began to make one change after another to the original formula. However, nothing he tried succeeded any better.

Eastman even moved into the factory to continue his experiments. Working night and day, stopping only to rest in a hammock strung up in the middle of the laboratory, he carried out a total of 469 experiments. Every single one of these experiments ended in failure. Could it be that he had quit his job at the bank too soon?

On March 12, 1882, George Eastman and Colonel Henry Strong sailed to England. The two partners must have made quite a picture—the middle-aged, heavyset Strong and the thin, energetic Eastman—as they strolled along the deck of the ship.

By this time, the colonel had invested $5,000 in the Eastman Dry Plate Company and most likely saw his future riding there rather than in buggy whips. In London, Eastman discussed the formula with the experts and bought new chemicals. This time he tested every chemical to make sure it was fresh and worked.

On April 4, when the two partners returned to the United States, Eastman could hardly wait to get back into the laboratory. The red fog that had streaked across the previous plates was no longer present. After sixteen further experiments, Eastman was satisfied that he could once again produce high-quality dry plates. The Eastman Dry Plate Company was back in business.

All along, the problem had not been with the formula but with the gelatin. Eastman had learned another very valuable lesson the hard way. He now knew how important it was to test everything he was going to use.

Moreover, he understood why it was important to "control the alternative." By this he meant that there should be more than one way of doing things. In the future, Eastman would make sure that there was an alternative available for everything that the company was manufacturing.

As Eastman began to think more and more about the future, he set forth certain principles that would serve as a practical guide throughout his long career:

1. Use machines to achieve large-scale production.
2. Sell at the lowest possible price.
3. Sell both in the United States and in foreign countries.
4. Advertise and demonstrate widely in order to increase sales.

As Eastman's first full year in the dry-plate business came to a close, the bookkeeping showed that the new company had pulled in $14,000. The business had grown so much that Eastman had to relocate to a three-story factory building.

Someone else might have been satisfied, but not George Eastman. He was already eagerly looking ahead to the next challenge. What he chose to tackle next was the development of something that could replace the glass plate: convenient-to-use flexible film. He wrote:

> I first conceived the process of making Transparent Film by coating a support with a solution of Nitro Cellulose, and then coating it with emulsion [a liquid mixture of silver halides] and afterwards stripping it off—early in the year 1884.... The experiments that I made produced films upon which I was able to make pictures by leaving the films upon the paper support during the exposure and development, and stripping them afterwards.

It was a delicate procedure of stripping away the paper and gelatin from the film on the glass plate that Eastman finally perfected. (This was one of the major reasons that Eastman would later start a full developing service for customers.) But when the emulsion that had dried on the plate was developed, it did not have any of the graininess of previous paper film. At last satisfied with the quality of this process, Eastman, on March 4, 1884, applied for a patent for American Film.

Perhaps it was not only the potential financial value of patents to the inventor, especially as shown by the misfortune of Frederick Scott Archer, that pushed Eastman to apply immediately for patents. One of George Eastman's closest friends in Rochester, George Selden, also happened to be a patent attorney.

Although flexible film may have been ready for cameras, cameras were not ready for flexible film. Cameras had backs that only accepted glass plates. Something had to be invented to replace the glass-plate holder.

This is an 1884 portrait of George Eastman, taken as an experiment with his new American Film. The writing says: "Made on paper with a soluble substratum developed after transferring. Feb 18/84"

In the beginning of 1884, Eastman hired William H. Walker, who had earlier designed cameras and managed a camera company. Working together, Eastman and Walker built a mahogany frame supporting two metal pins—one for the roll of film and the other for the take-up spool.

The Eastman-Walker roll holder not only held the strip of twenty-four-picture film; but also by turning a key, the film was advanced. When the film had been turned forward the right amount for the next frame, a small noise sounded. The roll holder could also be placed on the back of any standard camera. Now, photographers everywhere could use the lighter and more convenient film.

In the beginning, there were only a few photographers who switched to film. One who did so was William Henry Jackson, a documentary photographer of the Far West. He was a photographer for the U.S. Geological and Geographical Survey of the Territories. Jackson was no stranger to the difficulty of using glass plates in the field. To record a survey of the Oregon Trail in 1870, Jackson had hauled three large cameras and close to four hundred glass plates in a continual battle against rough rivers, weather, and mountains. In addition, in order to get the photographs he wanted, Jackson would often crisscross and backtrack three miles for every single mile actually traveled.

"I am a thousand times obliged to you for the beautiful holder sent me," an appreciative Jackson wrote Eastman, "but more for the new power placed in our hands whereby our labors are made sport. Truly our day of deliverance has come."

But unlike Jackson, most photographers were reluctant to use film because the results were so unpredictable. Even with this slow start, however, Eastman foresaw film as

PAPER DRY PLATES.

Fig. 1.

The EASTMAN DRY PLATE AND FILM COMPANY

are now ready to supply their new materials for making flexible negatives, as follows :

Improved Negative Paper, cut sheets in regular sizes.
Improved Negative Paper on spools, to fit the Eastman-Walker Roll Holder.
The Eastman-Walker Roll Holder, for making exposures on the continuous strip.
Film Carriers, for supporting single sheets of the negative paper in ordinary dark slides.

Fig. 2.   Fig. 3.

EASTMAN'S IMPROVED NEGATIVE PAPER,

prepared by a new method (patent applied for), gives negatives which print remarkably free from grain and as quick as the average dry plates. This paper has all the good qualities of glass dry plates, with only one-twentieth its weight or bulk. One gross of glass dry plates, 5x8, weighs 55 pounds, while one gross of paper, same size, packed, weighs less than two pounds and a quarter, and is free from liability of breakage during transportation. They can be used in any climate.

The development, fixing and washing are the same as for glass, except that a number may be operated upon at the same time in one dish.

After drying, the paper is rendered transparent in a simple and expeditious manner. Full directions with each package.

A full outfit for working this process consists of—

    1 Package of Negative Papers.
    2 Film Carriers.
    1 Squeegee.

Every photographer and every amateur should send for an outfit of such size as he may be able to use. One trial will show the superiority of the new negative paper.

Figure 1 shows the negative paper as put up on spools to fit the

EASTMAN-WALKER ROLL HOLDER.

Figure 2 shows the **Roll Holder,** with the case partly raised. Figure 3 shows the movement with case removed. Figure 4 shows the movement thrown back for insertion or withdrawal of spool of paper.

Fig. 4.

These Holders are made in such a manner as to enable any good wood-workman to fit them to any camera. In ordering, send outside measurement of plate holder.

Figure 5 shows **Film Carrier** for supporting single sheets in the ordinary holder, and the manner of putting in the paper.

Fig. 5.

An 1885 advertisement for the Eastman-Walker roll holder.

an important new direction for photography. To raise money for this new venture, Eastman reorganized the company. Instead of the name Eastman Dry Plate Company, it was now called the Eastman Dry Plate & Film Company of Rochester. This was the announcement for the new company:

> The Eastman Dry Plate & Film Company of Rochester incorporated Oct. 1st, 1884, paid up capital stock of $200,000, has purchased the plant and stock of the Eastman Dry Plate Company, and in addition to carrying on the manufacture of the well-known Eastman dry plates will introduce about January 1st a new paper dry plate which it is confidently expected will eventually displace the present glass plates.
>
> The new process will save Photographers about a quarter of a million dollars yearly on their dry-plate bills.
>
> The Company has also perfected and patented a roller holder which will reduce the weight of the apparatus required for outdoor photography about one half. The exposures being made upon a continuous strip which is afterwards cut up and developed, the resulting negatives being undistinguishable from those made upon glass.
>
> The officers of the new Company are:
>
> Henry A. Strong, President
>
> J. H. Kent, Vice   "
>
> George Eastman, Treasurer
>
> Wm. H. Walker, Secretary

Although Eastman may have been listed only as treasurer of the new company, he was really in charge of the day-to-day operations. For not only did he know more about the company's financial picture, but he also knew more about its technical and production side than any other person. He always stayed closely connected to the development of new products and to the opening up of new markets. He was totally involved in every aspect of the company. As Eastman once said about himself, "I made it my business to keep thoroughly posted."

In a letter to his brother-in-law in Cleveland (George W. Andrus had married Eastman's sister Ellen Maria), Eastman could barely contain his excitement. He wrote, "If the thing [the new company] is a partial success it will be a good thing while if it is a complete success it will dazzle the eyes of the gentle beholder."

Always alert to new ways to promote his own business as well as photography in general, Eastman shared his enthusiasm with the director of a photographic exhibition in London. "We shall be able to popularize photography," exclaimed Eastman, "to an extent as yet scarcely dreamed of."

As a matter of fact, the future popularity of photography would prove to be so overwhelming, it would come as a surprise even to the farseeing George Eastman.

5

Eastman and the Kodak Camera

Ａs George Eastman saw it, there were two basic problems in photography. One was with the film. Eastman
had already begun the movement away from heavy,
troublesome glass plates toward lighter, more trouble-free
film.

The other problem, it seemed to him, was with the
camera. Cameras were bulky, heavy, difficult to operate,
and expensive. Eastman wanted to develop cameras that
were small, light, easy to use, and cheap.

In the fall of 1885, working with Franklin M. Cossitt,
Eastman began a project to build what was referred to as a
detective camera. Detective cameras could supposedly be
used to take photographs without others knowing that
pictures were being taken.

One detective camera in particular was popular in
those days. It was hung around the neck and looked like a

round canteen peeking through the lapels of the photographer's jacket. Most of these cameras weren't really used secretively by detectives. It was just that these cameras were smaller than ordinary cameras. Detective cameras did not need to be balanced on tripods, either. Instead, they could be held in the hand.

Eastman had hoped his camera could be "put on the market at such a low price that it would be a leading card for us and defy competition from other makers." To make the camera economical, it would have to use film rather than glass plates. But film still had not been accepted by the public. Consequently, Eastman decided to use glass plates instead. Glass plates raised the price of Eastman and Cossitt's camera to fifty dollars, making their detective camera too expensive to produce.

Eastman was a person who knew when to give up and start over. So, for a small fee he sold all the cameras that had been finished to a photographic supply house and began again. By the same token, Eastman knew when to stand firm and put everything he had into something he believed in.

Perhaps Eastman knew these things because he had to grow up so quickly. He had learned how to consider all the facts, make a decision, and follow through. He had developed the sure instincts of someone confident and responsible. In short, George Eastman liked being in charge. "If you cannot run the business alone as far as these matters are concerned," Eastman once said, "you will certainly be no better off by letting four or five others dabble at it."

Eastman had also learned something else. The company was not selling very much roll film, but it was successful with its picture-enlarging service, developing large prints from negatives sent to it by customers. This was the opposite of what he might have expected. "When we started out with our scheme of film photography, we expected that everybody that used glass plates would take up films," admitted Eastman. "[B]ut we found that the number that did this was relatively small and that in order to make a large business we would have to reach the general public and create a new class of patrons."

Eastman decided that it was time to head off in a new direction. He hired Henry M. Reichenbach right off the campus of the Massachusetts Institute of Technology in Cambridge. When Eastman told Walker about his new chemist, it was clear that many of Eastman's future goals were long-term:

> We have a young chemist who devotes his time entirely to experiments and we hope he will strike the right emulsion sooner or later, but it may be a long job. He knows nothing about photography which was all the better. I told him what was wanted and that it might take a day, a week, a month or a year to get it or perhaps longer but that it was a dead sure thing in the end.

Another chemist, Frank W. Lovejoy, had "no knowledge of celluloid or of photography or of the...Company." Lovejoy not only was hired but even went on to become the fourth president of the company.

Eastman may have always been interested in making money, but he wanted to make it by delivering quality at a fair price.

George Eastman saw the future of photography as a shift away not only from the professional photographer but also from the serious amateur photographer. From now on the opportunity for growth would be to attract the average person, the person who had never even held a camera before. Eastman's goals were both long-range and short-range: to make photographers out of everyone.

However, George Eastman was also forming other goals. One of them involved education. In 1887, Eastman wrote out his first check for education, giving $50 to the Mechanics Institute of Rochester, a local trade school. Fifty dollars may not seem like a lot for a George Eastman, unless you stop to consider that as the treasurer of the company back then he had been making $60 a week. (To look at his salary from a different point of view, $60 a week was actually quite a handsome salary at that time when you realize that an unskilled worker earned about $60 a month. Also, $60 a week in 1887 translates to roughly $654 in 1992.)

Four years later, George Eastman gave the same school $5,000 toward their plan of buying property in order to relocate their school in downtown Rochester. "I believe that the best investment the manufacturers, merchants, and property owners of this city can make," wrote Eastman, "is to liberally endow [to give money or property that can serve as a permanent source of income] the Institute."

It was in the summer of 1887 that Eastman began work on a camera that would change photography forever. Unlike the detective camera, this new camera looked like a black shoebox, and more important, it was simple to manufacture.

Eastman's box camera was small. Its width and height measured less than four inches; its length measured less than seven inches. Eastman's box camera was light, weighing only twenty-two ounces. George Eastman's "pack-horse load" days had been left far behind.

Eastman's new camera was also easy to use. In order for the picture to be in focus, the subject had to be at least eight feet away. The camera had only one lens opening and one shutter speed. (The shutter is a mechanical device that opens to let in light and expose the film, and then closes again. The shutter did away with the need for a cap to be placed over the lens after each exposure.)

The camera came with a roll of film that could take a hundred round pictures two and a half inches in diameter. The film was advanced by turning a key until a mark showed that enough film had been turned for the next frame. When all one hundred pictures had been exposed, the entire camera was sent back to Rochester. There, in darkness, the film was unloaded, developed, printed, and reloaded.

The price of the camera was $25. The cost of developing and printing the film, as well as putting in a new roll of film, was another $10. While it may not have been exactly cheap, it was certainly less expensive than the $100 Eastman had spent when he started out in photography. Also, it was the working out of an idea that was becoming more and more attractive to Eastman: to provide the customer with a complete photographic service.

By June 1888, the new camera was finished. George Eastman must have cut quite a striking figure in his three-piece suit and closely cropped dark beard, smiling broadly under a new black derby. Did those who greeted him as he walked briskly down State Street realize that Eastman was on the road to a huge success? In their wildest imagination, could they have guessed that George Eastman was going to make the Eastman Kodak Company as well as Rochester famous all around the world?

For this fundamentally different camera and photographic system, George Eastman wanted to coin a brand-new word. "The elimination of the word 'camera' is a good thing and comes back to my original idea, to make a new word to express the whole thing...," he wrote. Eastman wanted a word that would not be confused with any other—a word that would be recognizable anywhere.

Eastman had always had a favorite letter, the letter *k*. It sounded "firm and unyielding." Also, it was the first letter of Kilbourn, his mother's birth family name. And two *k*'s were even better than one. Finally, Eastman came up with the brand name he had been searching for. He wrote:

> In regard to the word Kodak I can say that it was a purely arbitrary [subjective] combination of letters, not derived [handed down] in whole or part from any existing word, arrived at after considerable search for a word that would answer all requirements for a trade-mark name [a name used to distinguish one's goods from a competitor's]. The principal of these were that it must be short; incapable of being misspelled so as to destroy its identity; must have a vigorous and distinctive personality; and must meet the requirements of the various foreign trade-mark laws.

Even Eastman's partner tried the new camera. George Eastman must have smiled as he told the following story about Henry Strong: "I gave one of these cameras to Mr. Strong who took it with him on a trip to Tacoma on Puget Sound a few weeks ago. It was the first time he had ever carried a camera, and he was tickled with it as a boy over a new top. I never saw anybody so pleased...that it was a possible thing to take pictures himself."

In September 1888, the Kodak camera was ready for

This is the 1888 No. 1 Kodak camera.

shipping to stores. In addition to the usual photographic supply houses, the Kodak would also be sold in drugstores. This would make it available to many more people.

But Eastman was not happy about the instruction booklet. The advertising agency that had been hired to produce it had missed the whole point. Instead of making the camera sound simple, they had made it seem complicated. Needing the booklet immediately, Eastman sat down and wrote one in only five hours. It stated in part:

> *Yesterday* the photographer, whether he used glass plates or films, must have a dark room and know all about focusing, relation of lens apertures to light and spend days and weeks learning developing, fixing, intensifying, printing, toning, and mounting before he could show good results from his labors.

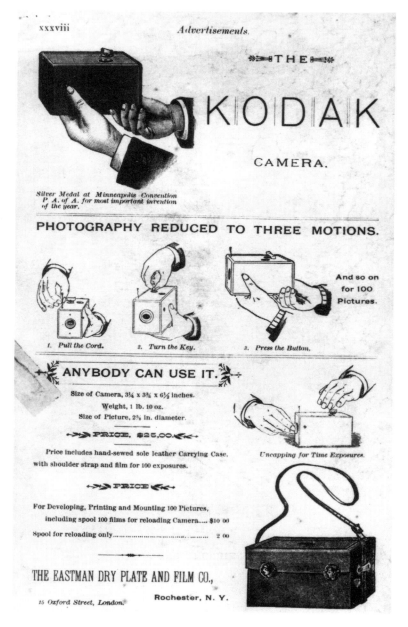

An 1889 advertisement for the new Kodak camera.

Today photography has been reduced to a cycle of three operations:

1.—Pull the String.   2.—Turn the Key.
3.—Press the Button.

Having done so well with the instruction booklet, Eastman now applied himself to the advertising campaign. But he was to outdo even himself by putting everything that needed to be said about this new photographic approach into just one sentence. Indeed, this turned out to be one of the most successful ad campaigns ever developed. Simple, to the point, and once heard easily remembered, the world-famous slogan of the Kodak company became

YOU PRESS THE BUTTON
WE DO THE REST

A year after the Kodak hit the market, 13,000 cameras had been sold, and every day 70 rolls of film were being processed.

"The craze," announced the *Chicago Tribune*, "is spreading fearfully.... Chicago has had many fads whose careers have been brilliant but brief. But when amateur photography came, it came to stay."

This turned out to be a more accurate prediction than that made by Alfred Stieglitz, a famous photographer whose photographs are still popular. "[P]hotography as a fad is well-nigh on its last legs, thanks principally to the bicycle craze."

The new film used in the Kodaks was called American Film—a film that had to be stripped from its paper backing and developed on glass plates. However, Reichenbach and the film department were carrying out experiments using nitrocellulose. (Nitrocellulose was a flammable substance formed by the action of nitric acid on cellulose.) Their goal was to develop a film made of celluloid—a strong, transparent plastic.

By 1889 the Eastman Dry Plate & Film Company held a patent for a celluloid film. However, there were several other companies trying to take away control of the market or at least gain a part of it.

"The new film is the 'slickest' product that we ever tried to make," observed Eastman about celluloid film, "and its method of manufacture will eliminate all of the defects hitherto experienced in film manufacture. . . . If we can fully control it I would not trade it for the telephone. [Alexander Graham Bell had invented the telephone in 1876.] There is more millions in it than anything else because the patents are young and the field won't require 8 or 10 years to develop it & introduce it."

On December 24, 1889, the Eastman Company was incorporated, replacing the Eastman Dry Plate & Film Company.

In a continual search for larger quarters, George Eastman had for years been moving his company from one building to another in downtown Rochester. Finally, in 1890, Eastman bought land three miles away. Construction began immediately on a film factory, a laboratory, and a power plant. From 1891 on, most of the buildings of the Eastman Company would be located in this area that came to be known as Kodak Park.

In 1892, Eastman built a factory for a thousand workers on State Street called the Camera Works. Then he rented it to Frank Brownell, a camera designer who had been working for Eastman since 1885. Eastman felt fortunate about this association with Brownell, calling him "the greatest camera designer that ever lived." In his seventeen-year career at Kodak, Frank Brownell would be responsible for designing no fewer than sixty different types of Kodak cameras.

In 1889, two more Kodaks had been released. The No. 1 Kodak was basically Eastman's original Kodak with an improved shutter. The No. 2 Kodak was bigger and more suitable for professionals. It used film that made sixty pictures with a diameter of 3 ½ inches.

The next year saw the No. 3 Kodak, a camera that produced negatives in the shape of a rectangle, and the No. 4 Kodak, the first of many popular folding Kodaks. Attached by an accordion-type part that could expand and fold up, the lens pulled out when in use and folded back when not in use, making the camera more compact.

ABC Kodaks, using film that could be loaded in broad daylight, were introduced in 1891. (The name referred to the simplicity of their use, "as simple as ABC.") No longer would it be necessary to send cameras back to Rochester to be unloaded and reloaded. These loaded-when-needed, lightweight cameras were similar in function to cameras used today.

On May 23, 1892, the official name of the business was changed from the Eastman Company to the Eastman Kodak Company.

The "Pocket Kodak" came out in 1895. This small, lightweight camera was easy to use and extremely popular. One hundred thousand were sold in the very first year.

Kodak also brought out a camera called the Bullet in 1895. It not only used film that could be loaded in broad daylight but also stretched the film across the front of the camera. The absence of the roll holder made the camera lighter, and there was less distortion (the image out of proportion) in the photograph when it was printed. The problem with the Bullet was that it was a copy of another camera, the Bull's-Eye, made by a company in Boston.

Over the years, there were many fights between Kodak and other companies over patents. At times these were patents of cameras, at other times of film. Sometimes Kodak was found to be in the right; sometimes Kodak was found to be in the wrong. But whatever the situation or the outcome, George Eastman was never afraid of lawsuits. He had a fierce fighting spirit.

The camera that was to capture the hearts and minds of people was a Kodak box camera known as the Brownie. Most likely a nickname in honor of its creator, Frank Brownell, the first Brownie was sold in 1900. The last Brownie, an updated version of the original, was still on the market almost eighty years later.

One of the big reasons the Brownie caught on so quickly was the price. It only cost one dollar. At fifteen cents a roll, the film was no less of a bargain. "Photography," noted Eastman, "is thus brought within reach of every human being who desires to preserve a record of what he sees."

The Brownie was advertised as a camera ideal for children. Ads in the popular magazines of the day showed a drawing of "The Brownie Boy" bouncing across the page. Other ads displayed a photograph of "The Brownie Girl." She was a grinning girl on a beach, wearing a broad-brimmed hat, skirt, and jacket, looking as if she were ready to take a picture of the reader.

During the first year of production, more than 250,000 Brownies were sold. Although aimed at children, the Brownie was a camera ideal for people of all ages.

"Now every nipper has a Brownie and a photograph is as common as a box of matches," complained Alvin Langdon Coburn, a professional photographer. Later Coburn would abandon taking straightforward photographs in favor of abstract and cubist images. "Why should not the camera artist break away from the worn-out conventions, that...restrict his medium," asked Coburn, "and claim the freedom of expression which any art must have to be alive?"

Alfred Stieglitz registered a very different kind of reaction to the wide availability of cameras. "Don't believe you became an artist the instant you received a gift Kodak on Xmas morning," he warned.

But one of the first greats of photography, Nadar (whose real name was Gaspard-Félix Tournachon) had long before, in 1857, addressed the threat of the amateur:

> The theory of photography can be learnt in an hour; the first ideas of how to go about it in a day. What can't be learnt...is the feeling for light—the artistic appreciation of effects produced by different or combined sources; it's the understanding of this or that effect following the lines of the features which requires your artistic perception [awareness and insight].

Even before Eastman's inventions, the rise of photography affected the other arts. Although it had once been predicted ("from today painting is dead" declared artist Paul Delaroche), the invention of the daguerreotype did not mean the end of painting. Instead, photography broadened the range of what artists could do. It helped artists to see things differently. Different angles, different

shapes, different interplays of light and dark, different ways of establishing the borders of a painting—these were some of the many influences of photography on painting.

Much of the last hundred years of art can even be viewed in the light of photography. Some art has been directly influenced by photography. Take, for example, the paintings of the photo-realists in recent years. These are paintings painted directly from photographs. Sometimes, the artist will even project the photograph onto the canvas. Other art has been a rejection of photography, such as the abstract art that covers many of the walls of museums of modern art. Abstract art explores ideas such as form, color, and movement. It does not attempt to represent the world pictorially, the way a photographer might.

Photography has also had a powerful impact on writing. Émile Zola, a French writer in the latter part of the 1800s, was famous for his realistic fiction. In his novels, he piled on detail after detail. Zola was also a Sunday-afternoon-in-the-park-type photographer. "You cannot say you have thoroughly seen anything until you have got a photograph of it," noted Zola, "revealing a lot of points which otherwise would be unnoticed, and which in most cases could not be distinguished."

This photographic way of seeing "a lot of points which otherwise would be unnoticed" can be glimpsed in the opening scene of *Nana*, a novel of Zola's published in 1880. It was as if the writer had used a camera to take photographs all over the inside of a theater:

At nine o'clock in the evening the body of the house at the Theatre des Varietes was still all but empty. A few individuals, it is true, were sitting quietly waiting in the balcony and stalls, but these were lost, as it were, among the ranges of seats whose coverings of cardinal velvet loomed in the subdued light of the dimly-burning lustre. A shadow enveloped the great red splash of the curtain, and not a sound came from the stage, the unlit footlights, the scattered desks of the orchestra.

The realism of Zola also influenced a group of writers in the United States. One of them was Stephen Crane. Crane's best-known work is *The Red Badge of Courage: An Episode of the American Civil War.* Published in 1895 when the author was only twenty-four, this short novel details the change of a raw recruit, Henry Fleming, into a seasoned veteran:

As he hastened, there passed through his mind pictures of stupendous conflicts. His accumulated thought upon such subjects was used to form scenes....

He came to a fence and clambered over it. On the far side, the ground was littered with clothes and guns. A newspaper, folded up, lay in the dirt. A dead soldier was stretched with his face hidden in his arm. Farther off there was a group of four or five corpses keeping mournful company. A hot sun had blazed upon the spot.

The language in Crane's book is so realistic, immediate, and visual—almost photographic in describing scenes—that today's readers are sometimes surprised to find out that Stephen Crane had not actually witnessed the Civil War; he was born six years after it had ended. Viewing the photographs of Mathew Brady, the famous

Civil War photographer, was probably the closest Crane came to the war.

By the end of the nineteenth century, thousands of ordinary Americans had begun to use Eastman's cameras and film to take photographs. These pictures were not considered artwork but were called snapshots.

What is a snapshot? A snapshot is a photo that is snapped, or shot quickly. Most likely it's made with little thought about technique. It's a quick record of an event, a gathering of people, a scene that grabs one's interest. For instance, one might snap a neighbor at a graduation ceremony proudly wearing cap and gown, a grandparent gingerly holding a grandchild, a blaze of sunset gradually settling behind a mountain.

In describing an album of snapshots, George Eastman said, "Such a photographic notebook is an enduring record of many things seen only once in a lifetime and enables the fortunate possessor to go back by the light of his own fireside to scenes which would otherwise fade from memory and be lost."

It is due to cameras like the Brownie that cameras have become commonplace and that countless snapshots spill out of private albums everywhere. Eastman had a dream "to make Kodakers of every school boy or girl and every wage-earning man and woman the world over."

Later, Eastman purchased the patent needed to develop what would perhaps be the ideal camera for the snapshot craze. Called the Autographic Kodak, this camera was first put on the market in 1914. The idea behind it was that no one would ever have to look through a pile of snapshots again and wonder when and where a picture had been taken and who was in it.

After taking the picture, a small door could be pulled

open and the important details written right at the bottom of the negative. Later, these would appear on the developed and printed snapshot. Realizing that "all these things add to the value of the picture," Eastman brought out twenty different models of the Autographic Kodak over a twenty-year period.

It was Eastman's belief that "[a] collection of these pictures may be made to furnish a pictorial history of life as it is lived by the owner, that will grow more valuable every day that passes."

Of the millions and millions of photographs that have been taken, most are snapshots. "Most photographs are made for the purpose of obtaining a record which cannot be had in any other way," George Eastman recognized. "When the desire for a pictorial record of daily life disappears, then amateur photography will decrease, and not until then."

6

A Close-up of the Eastman Kodak Company

Over the years, thousands of people worked for George Eastman. Of the many employees at Kodak Park, one of the most important was George Eastman's personal secretary, Alice E. Whitney Hutchison. Serving more like a chief of staff as she screened calls and offered advice, Whitney was the type of employee Eastman prized the most: a person who was not only loyal and hardworking but would spend an entire career working for Kodak. Hired in 1890, Mrs. Alice Whitney Hutchison was to stay on at Kodak Park for more than forty years.

Another long-term employee, Joseph Thacher Clarke, traveled all over the world for Kodak. Eastman had first met Clarke in 1886. Clarke had experience in designing cameras, but more than that, the two men saw eye to eye on many important issues. In addition, they just plain liked each other.

Eastman hired Clarke to be the "scientific expert for Europe," but actually, he was a roving troubleshooter for the company. That meant that during his thirty-four-year career with the company he would go wherever his problem-solving skills might be needed.

What was it like to work for George Eastman? F. W. Krohn, a chemist at the Kodak Company in England, explained it this way:

"He never for one moment let you feel other than absolutely natural with him. Is it wonderful then that it did not take you long to feel not only a great respect for him,

George Eastman and his Kodak camera aboard ship on one of his transatlantic business trips.

but great affection and absolute loyalty? I never saw Mr. Eastman in a temper. You therefore knew instinctively that he could control and lead men for he possessed the first essential of a great leader, control of himself."

In contrast to his experiences with Alice Whitney Hutchison, Joseph Thacher Clarke, and F. W. Krohn, George Eastman had experiences with other employees who were far from loyal or hardworking.

In 1887, Franklin M. Cossitt, a foreman and an operator of the continuous coating paper machine for producing bromide paper, disappeared along with David Cooper, a traveling salesman. Later, they turned up at the Anthony Company trying to duplicate the machinery used by the Kodak Company. Eastman filed a lawsuit. The employees were fired by Anthony, and the machinery was never used.

William Walker, one of the original officers in the company, was sent to London to head the Eastman company there. However, Walker's management style of both feet propped up on the desk soon became a problem. The company in England ran into problem after problem, not the least of which was losing money. In addition, Walker and Eastman differed in their business outlooks. Walker was more interested in a quick, modest profit, whereas Eastman thought in terms of long-range goals in order to achieve a colossal success. In 1893, Eastman encouraged Walker to accept early retirement.

In April 1892, Henry Reichenbach had helped Eastman to solve the important problem of eliminating the electricity in movie film. Soon afterward, however, it was discovered that Reichenbach and two other employees were going to use secret Kodak formulas to start a rival company. Eastman quickly fired Reichenbach and the other two.

Seventeen years later, in 1909, Henry Reichenbach brazenly applied for another job at Kodak. Eastman was quick to respond.

My Dear Henry:
On my return home from several weeks' absence I find yours of Mar. 19th. While I do not now cherish any ill feelings towards you on account of the past I think you can see that it would be impossible for me to give you employment in the Company on account of the influence it would have. With best wishes, I remain,
Yours very truly,
Geo. Eastman

There was one hiring and firing in particular that shows how demanding and unsentimental Eastman could be when he felt it was necessary. After Reichenbach's dismissal, Kodak needed a good worker to make film coatings called emulsions. (An emulsion is the mixture of silver halides used to coat the film.) George Eastman learned that George Monroe, his former photography teacher, was successfully making emulsions for the Hammer Dry Plate Company of St. Louis, Missouri. So, Eastman recruited and hired the man who had taught him about wet-plate photography.

At first, everything went well. However, George Monroe and Darragh de Lancey, the manager of Kodak Park, could not get along. Rivalries developed among other employees, and morale declined. When reports of spoiled film started to roll in, Eastman quickly let Monroe go.

Although George Eastman may not have been an easy person to work for, he demanded no less from others than he expected from himself. And what he expected from himself was something closely akin to perfection—or as close to it as he could manage to get.

On the other hand, Eastman could help out someone that others might easily have turned their backs on. Just such a person was Samuel N. Turner.

Turner had invented a daylight-loading spool that Eastman needed in order for Kodak to build a folding camera. Eastman offered a royalty, which is a percentage payment, in this case to an inventor, for each item sold. If the item sells well, the inventor who receives royalty payments can make a lot of money over the years. If not many items are sold, the inventor can earn very little since the royalties would be small. But instead of accepting royalty payments over the years, Turner requested and was paid a lump sum.

Years later, Turner sued Eastman. During the court case, Turner signed an affidavit, or sworn written statement, in which he declared that he had not really invented the spool. It was an extremely curious statement for Turner to make, for Turner's patent was immediately declared invalid. The grounds for the lawsuit melted away.

In 1919, Eastman heard that Turner had gone through all his money and was living in poverty. Having always believed that Turner really had invented the spool, Eastman came to his aid. Turner was put on a Kodak pension for the rest of his life.

What was George Eastman like? He was only five feet nine inches tall, but his broad shoulders made him seem bigger. And from the age of forty he had gray hair. He did have friends, although there remained about George Eastman an air of formality. Quite simply, he was not an easy person to get to know.

Colonel Henry Alvah Strong, one of Eastman's oldest

friends, once wrote a letter to him (addressed to "Dear Skinny") that ended on this personal note: "I know you never want any sympathy or comfort from your friends... but I want you to know that *I*, for one, appreciate the mountains of care and responsibility that you are constantly called upon to overcome.... I sometimes think that we do not know each other very well, anyhow. We surely are neither of us very demonstrative."

This formality and reserve may have caused people to think George Eastman was distant and cold, or it may have prevented people from trying to become close friends with him. However, there certainly were many people, particularly his long-standing partner, who cared deeply about Eastman.

Once when troubles seemed to be multiplying, Strong offered these kind words of encouragement: "Keep a stiff upper lip and do not lose sight of the fact that if the emulsion goes wrong, plates fog, the Solio [one of Eastman's papers for printing pictures] turns yellow and the Bromide paper blisters, all of these troubles will disappear after a while."

George Eastman never married. Here are a few possible reasons.

Eastman had always worked so hard that he may not have allowed the time needed to meet, date, and marry someone. He seemed to have little time to spend in the social situations that many other young people of Rochester enjoyed. Business *was* his private life.

Perhaps it was because Eastman had been so devoted to his mother. Eastman had stepped in to fill his father's shoes and help lessen the financial burdens of the family. When Eastman began his own business, there were the years of building up the business and then his many projects to help others. There was always something to take up his time. Years later, Eastman remarked: "All I had in mind was to make enough money so that my mother would never have to work again." Then again, his mother and his two sisters may have been all the family he felt he ever really needed.

However, when Eastman was seventeen, he had at least considered the possibility of marriage. In a letter to Mary Eastman, a cousin in Ohio, Eastman had written: "How is Cousin Carrie? Has she commenced that tidy [decorative covering to protect the back or arms of a chair] she was going to make for me when I got married? Tell her to make it alike on both sides."

In his mid-twenties, Eastman had recorded in the notebook he kept with him the various times when he had taken one of the three young women he occasionally dated to the roof of the Powers Building—the seven-story "sky-scraper" where young people went on a summer's evening in Rochester.

Perhaps it may never have occurred to Eastman that he wasn't going to get married. He had simply always been too busy to think about it. Then one day it may have dawned on him that he probably never would marry—that he was going to skip over to the age of a grandfather without ever having been a father. And like many a person who stays single for years and years, Eastman may have become firmly set in his ways. In any case, he seemed to enjoy his life just the way it was. George Eastman led a busy, eventful, and full life.

In 1898 the British subsidiary (a subsidiary is a company owned by another company) Kodak Limited was established with a total value of $8 million. The Eastman Kodak Company was a business controlling Kodak companies around the world. George Eastman, in his mid-forties, became a millionaire. ("Mother, we have a million dollars now," Eastman excitedly told his mother. "That's nice, George," was Maria Eastman's reply.) In the first year or two of the Eastman Dry Plate Company, Strong had invested in the company by simply handing Eastman the money. Now, stock in the corporation would be sold in downtown Rochester. Anyone who wanted to invest in the company would be able to.

Eastman wanted to share some of this good fortune with his loyal employees, not as a gift but as "extra pay for extra good work." How much they received was determined by how long they had worked for Kodak and what their salary was. In any case, in 1899, $178,000 was divided among the 3,000 employees.

Money was only one of the rewards that Eastman presented to his employees. "The ideal large corporation," Eastman believed, "is one that makes the best use of the brains within it." In 1908, there were over 6,000 employees in his company. Only a few of the 375 managers had been brought in from the outside. Almost all of them had been promoted from within the company. Eastman encouraged promotions within the company because he had found out what it was like to be next in line for a job and not get it.

"My superior, whose assistant I was, left the bank," recalled Eastman. "The thing that I expected was that I should naturally fall in line for promotion. I didn't get it. Some relative of a director of the bank was brought in and placed over me. It wasn't right. It wasn't fair."

In 1911, Eastman began to explore setting up accident insurance and old-age pensions for his employees. In addition, he wanted a stock ownership program so that workers could buy stock in the company.

In 1912, Eastman also began for Kodak employees one of the first profit-sharing plans in the United States. The profits would not only go to the owners; some of the profits would be shared with the workers. His reasoning was that "employees engaged in an industry that is paying extraordinary dividends to its share holders are entitled to some recognition outside their fixed wage."

Eastman also shortened the workweek from fifty-four to fewer than fifty hours. On the other hand, George Eastman opposed a minimum wage law. He felt that such a law would raise prices for everything else as well. Consequently, Eastman believed workers would be no better off than they were in the beginning.

Over the years, there were many opportunities for Eastman to drive up prices. As his business empire grew and grew, more and more small companies could not stay in step with the equipment and services that Kodak offered. So, many of them went out of business.

Even the place that had first sold Eastman's dry plates, the Anthony and Scovill Company, offered to sell out to Eastman for $2 million. (Anthony, the New York City company, had finally joined its long-time competitor, Scovill, originally of Waterbury, Connecticut.) The officers of Anthony and Scovill told Eastman that he could make that sum of money back in sixty days simply by raising prices.

But Eastman did not believe in doing business that way. Rather than driving competitors out of business and then raising prices, Eastman's goal was to outperform as well as to undersell all his rivals. Eastman was fiercely competitive. "Peace extends only to private life," he once declared. "In business it is war all the time."

Eastman Kodak would make money simply by doing a

larger volume of business than everyone else did. As George Eastman had once stated: "The manifest destiny of the Eastman Kodak Company is to be the largest manufacturer of photographic materials in the world, or else to go to pot."

"In the case of cameras," reasoned Eastman, "the first Kodak was sold for $25.00. The limit of competition between dealers would have made the minimum price $22.50. At the present time a camera much better in every respect except the covering of the case is sold for $2.00."

On several occasions Eastman did buy companies, primarily to avoid lawsuits because of patent infringements, that is, the violating of patent rights. One lawsuit in particular brought against Eastman was to prove especially costly. In 1902, the Ansco Company (ironically, the former Anthony and Scovill Company) sued Eastman Kodak for a patent violation involving flexible, transparent roll film made of nitrocellulose.

The Reverend Hannibal Goodwin had applied for his patent for a transparent film in 1887. But because of delay after delay and refiling application after application, it was not granted until 1898. During the 1880s Henry Reichenbach had developed a similar kind of flexible, transparent roll film. In 1889 Reichenbach applied for and received a patent. Apparently no one at Kodak had seen Goodwin's patent application. In addition, even after Ansco acquired Goodwin's patent, Ansco never developed it so that it could be used to manufacture film. Nevertheless, after a long and complicated lawsuit, Eastman Kodak in 1913 was judged guilty of patent infringement and fined $5 million.

Later, Eastman showed he was not one to hold a grudge. In 1920, when the Ansco Company was having financial trouble, Eastman volunteered to help. "[W]e are not only willing but would be very glad to furnish any assistance [to Ansco] that we can," said Eastman, "but in such a case it must be understood that we are not to receive any compensation or have any control of the business. We realize that we cannot be without competition and that any disaster coming to our largest competitor would be a disadvantage to us."

On the other hand, perhaps George Eastman just wanted to make a favorable impression on the U.S. government, which at that time was cracking down on trusts. A trust was a combination of businesses or corporations formed by a legal agreement. At that time many trusts were organized to reduce or end business competition.

In 1901 there were fourteen camera companies, and Eastman's company was by far the largest. By 1913 Kodak was doing even better because the motion picture industry needed so much of Eastman's celluloid safety film. Even when the motion picture industry returned to using the cheaper nitrocellulose film, Eastman still maintained his position as the major supplier.

Eastman's way of doing business was to deliver high-quality photographic equipment and film at a fair price. To achieve this policy, Eastman bought companies when necessary to avoid lawsuits on patent infringements and set the price that Kodak would sell goods to dealers. Eastman believed that price-cutting not only hurt the business owner but also the consumer. According to Eastman, in the end price-cutting would result in people's receiving less for their money.

In 1911, the U.S. government began an investigation of Eastman Kodak for violations of the Sherman Antitrust Act of 1890. This law, passed by Congress, was supposed to ban the formation of trusts and monopolies—business combinations that prevented competition. In 1913, the government filed a lawsuit. In 1915, Judge John R. Hazel of the U.S. Circuit Court of Appeals ruled that Eastman Kodak had established a monopoly, almost total control of an industry by one company. There were three reasons given. Eastman Kodak had restrictive contracts with paper companies; it had bought companies to eliminate the competition; and it had fixed prices.

Eastman Kodak appealed the decision. The final judgment came in 1921. Eastman Kodak was forced to sell six of its photographic companies and was not allowed to buy any more. Also, it was forbidden to fix the prices used for selling photographic equipment and supplies to dealers. Through it all, though, Eastman Kodak maintained a lion's share of the market.

In spite of these setbacks, Eastman's explanation of the overall success of the Eastman Kodak Company was quite straightforward and simple. He wrote: "The fact is that we absolutely created the art of film photography and that we started from 80% to 90% of the customers on our books in the business of selling photographic goods."

Kodak had become so closely associated with photography that the name itself could almost be used in place of the words *camera* or *film*. It was a bit like someone asking, "Do you have a Kleenex?" Although Kleenex is a brand name, in people's thinking it is often substituted for facial tissue in general.

How closely associated the word *Kodak* had become with the field of photography can be seen in one of the Eastman Kodak Company's advertising slogans of the day: "If it isn't an Eastman, it isn't a Kodak."

7

The Development of Motion Pictures

One morning in the late spring of 1889, a mail sack was pulled open, and the following letter tumbled out. Eastman was certainly not in the habit of seeing individual orders from the many thousands that poured into the Eastman company. But he was shown this one:

Orange, N.J. May 30, 1889

The Eastman Dry Plate Co.,
Rochester, N.Y.

GENTLEMEN:
    Please quote us discount upon your Kodak camera, you list price, $25.00. Also discount upon reloading camera, list price $10.00.
Yours truly,
Edison Phonograph Works,
T. A. E.

The mysterious initials at the bottom of this letter proved to belong to none other than Thomas Alva Edison. Edison had already developed many inventions, including various types of telegraphs, the mimeograph, the microphone, the phonograph, and the incandescent electric light. But why should one of the leading inventors in the United States be interested in the Kodak camera? Edison sought the camera and the celluloid film in order to construct his very first motion picture camera.

In the 1870s, Eadweard Muybridge (pronounced ED-ward MY-brij), who had moved from England to the United States when a child, had begun to record several series of photographs. His studies in chronophotography (time photography) of galloping horses and of walking, running, wrestling, standing, and sitting people were the forerunners of the motion picture.

To photograph the galloping horse, Muybridge had used from twelve to twenty-four cameras set up along the horse's path. As the horse ran past each checkpoint, the shutter of a camera was triggered. By the use of this technique, Muybridge had even been able to prove that a galloping horse has all four feet off the ground at the same instant. (Muybridge's research also led to today's photo finish to help decide close races.)

After developing and printing these dry-plate photographs, Muybridge achieved a look of motion by arranging the photographs in order. His eleven-volume *Animal Locomotion,* published in 1887, contained some 20,000 individual images of humans and animals in motion.

Muybridge also displayed sequences of photographs in the whirling zoopraxiscope, so that the viewer saw what appeared to be movement due to something known as the persistence of vision. (This term means that the brain holds an image, in this case, of a photograph, even after it has been replaced by another photograph.) Consequently, a series of closely related images can give the appearance of movement. Basically, the zoopraxiscope presented a feeling of motion similar to the one you get with a children's flip book. As you press the book against your thumb and quickly release the pages, each flipped page shows a slightly different picture that blends with the pictures on the flipped pages before and after it.

In January 1888, Thomas Edison and his assistant, William Kennedy Laurie Dickson, met with Muybridge. The quantity and quality of Muybridge's work staggered them. When these two inventors returned to Edison's laboratory in West Orange, New Jersey, they set to work with renewed vigor.

The next letter Eastman received from the Edison Phonograph Works was on September 2, 1889:

> Dear Sirs:
>
> Enclosed please find sum of $2.50 P.O.O. [post office order] due you for one roll Kodak film for which please accept thanks—I shall try same to-day & report—it looks splendid—I never succeeded in getting this substance in such straight & long pieces—
> > Sincerely yrs.
> > W.K.L. Dickson
>
> Can you coat me some rolls of your highest sensitometer—please answer.

Following the receipt of this letter, long hours, days, weeks, and months of experimentation went on in Room Number Five in West Orange, New Jersey, as well as at Kodak Park in Rochester.

On July 23, 1891, George Eastman wrote to Henry Reichenbach, who was then Eastman's chief chemist in the film department:

Enclosed is a small fragment of film furnished Edison for his phonograph arrangement. [Edison originally thought that the motion picture would be based on the phonograph, his invention of 1877.] He perforates [makes holes in] it on both edges and delivers it by means of cog wheels. The film has to move 40 times a second and the movement has to be made in $1/10$ of the time.... The trouble with the film we have sent him is that the cogs tear the film slightly, as you will see by the enclosed, and gives blurred edges. I gave the Edison representative a sample of the double coated film made last August and told him if heavy enough we could furnish him that if he would take a whole table at a time in 41 inch strips.... Edison now has an order in for some narrow strips of film of our regular make. Please fill this and use the thickest skin that you can find.

On December 8, 1891, Eastman urged his chemist to work even harder. He wanted Reichenbach to realize the significance of his efforts. A very important race was underway among many companies in both the United States and in Europe, a race Eastman very much wanted to win.

"It is quite necessary that we should perfect our method for making double coated film," Eastman told Reichenbach. Then Eastman turned his attention to the biggest problem. "I think that if you persist in your experiments you can get rid of the electricity."

During April 1892 Reichenbach achieved success. Displaying the reasoning ability of a Sherlock Holmes, George Eastman launched into an explanation to William Walker of the mystery of the electricity that had been causing streaks on the film.

"One day, reflecting upon the theory that the discharge was caused by two surfaces, one of which was positive and the other negative, it occurred to me that if one of the surfaces was metallic there could be no generation. The idea of making one of the surfaces metallic naturally followed," reasoned Eastman. "A little further reflection, however, staggered me, because it seemed that the emulsion must be metallic...."

Collecting his thoughts, Eastman carefully continued:

Thinking about this matter convinced me that if the gelatine substratum [the thin coating on film for the emulsion to stick to] which we were then experimenting with, could be rendered a conductor at all it would not be by the use of any insoluble matter [something that cannot be dissolved]. I then naturally thought of the soluble salts and knowing that nitrates would not interfere with the emulsion [the light-sensitive layer], I decided to try them first. I directed Reichenbach to try the first experiment with Ammonium Nitrate, but he tried it with Potassium Nitrate, and found it worked perfectly.

For a public school dropout, Eastman could certainly put on a flashy display of reasoning. In addition, George Eastman could be counted on to understand the importance of being a major supplier of film to a movie industry. Early on he realized that "[t]he film business has the greatest possibilities of profit of any branch of photography and we must try to cover every avenue that leads to it."

Finally, in 1907, the two giants of the growing motion picture industry met for the first time. In the beginning, Eastman and Edison simply held each other in high regard. Later on, they would become friends.

At their meeting, Edison wanted to know how much film Eastman was selling to the Pathé Company in France. As usual, Edison was worried about his competitors in America and Europe. Eastman laughed aloud when Edison wondered if it might be as much as forty-five miles a day. But it was a guess not far off the mark. Pathé was certainly buying much more film than Edison was.

"I told Mr. Edison that I did not believe it would be a good thing for him to try to monopolize the whole cine business (producing, distributing, and exhibiting)," recalled Eastman of the meeting. "That in order to give it its full development it needed several minds to originate the great variety of subjects required."

The next major advance of the Eastman Kodak Company in the development of film came in 1908 with the development of a film made of cellulose acetate rather than nitrocellulose. There had already been several serious theater fires started by nitrocellulose film catching on fire while in the projector. The advantage of cellulose acetate film was that it was not flammable. It was a safety film.

No other company in America or in Europe was able to produce safety film. This meant that Eastman had the field all to himself. The demand for Eastman's film skyrocketed. Cellulose acetate film began to be produced in Kodak Park around the clock—twenty-four hours a day, seven days a week.

In 1895, Thomas Edison had introduced the kinetoscope. Strollers along the boardwalk and visitors to penny arcades (amusement centers with coin-operated games) could pay to view minute-long movies shot on fifty-foot strips of Eastman's film. From this humble beginning grew the glamorous motion picture industry.

As the scene shifted from penny arcades along boardwalks to theaters showing motion pictures, Eastman had cornered the film market, but Edison had a lock on the cameras and projectors. For instance, Edison had bought two patents that were indispensable to the manufacture of movie projectors. One was for the invention known as the

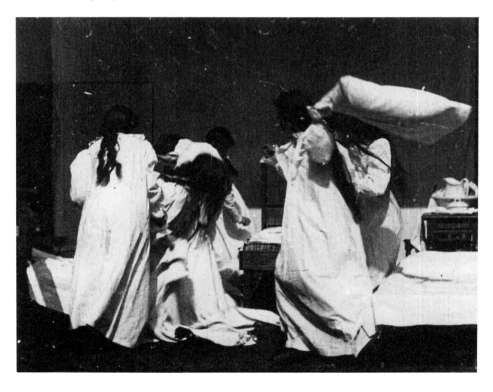

A film frame of a pillow fight scene in one of Thomas A. Edison's short kinetoscope motion pictures.

"Latham loop." This looped the film before it passed in front of the lens to reduce the stress on the film. Another was for an invention called the "Maltese cross." This was a simple but necessary contraption to cut down on the flickering of the image on the screen. With these two patents Edison tightened his grip on the motion picture industry.

Why was there all the fuss about patents and monopolies? Motion pictures had incredible possibilities. And the more advances there were in technology, the more money that could be made at the box office.

One of the first films to begin to display what was possible was a twelve-minute film called *The Great Train Robbery.* Made by the Edison Company in 1903, it was

This famous chase scene from The Great Train Robbery, *the 1903 Edison film classic, shows the robbers gaining on the train.*

directed by Edwin S. Porter, a former camera operator.

The story was simple enough. A band of robbers hop aboard a train, steal bags of money from the mail car, jump off the train, and are hunted down by a posse. It was a chase film containing the notion that crime doesn't pay.

This 800-foot-long strip of film is the granddaddy of a lot of action-packed films of the present day. One of the stunning techniques that Porter used is now called the intercut. This is the cutting, or alternating, from one camera angle to a contrasting camera angle. Although cutting from one camera shot to another is commonplace in every film nowadays, back then it was a novel way to view a scene.

Eastman had a contrasting view of his own to Edison's quest for monopoly of the industry. He wrote: "[T]he best thing for us to do is to bring our products up to the very highest state of perfection and reduce our price when we have to." Besides, Eastman was not only selling to Edison, the Pathé Company, the Biograph Company, and the other six film companies that formed what was called the Trust (nine companies that had agreed not to sell or rent equipment to any outside film companies). Eastman was also selling to the independents, those companies that were not part of the Trust.

Besides the high quality of his film, Eastman also stressed consistency. "It is not that anybody cannot make the same kind of film," stated Eastman from his headquarters at Kodak Park in Rochester, "but it is making film exactly the same everyday, and the man that can do it must get the trade, because there is so much dependent upon it."

As motion pictures caught on, they were becoming so profitable that the number of independent film companies grew. However, it wasn't easy for these independents. Not only did their camera equipment have to come all the way from Europe (because of Edison's patents), they also had to be on the lookout for thugs hired by the Trust while shooting their movies. A bullet hole through a camera could quickly put an independent film company out of business.

After the ever-popular *The Great Train Robbery,* another film to point out the possibilities of what motion pictures were capable of was D. W. Griffith's *The Birth of a Nation.*

Griffith had originally been a director for Biograph. In fact, he had been amazingly busy there, making over 450 films in only six years. Although Griffith would have been the first to admit that few of these films were works of art, many of them were money-makers.

Completed in 1915, *The Birth of a Nation* proved to be different from earlier films. It was an epic film in both concept and execution. Instead of being only one reel, the movie was spread out over four reels. Instead of being shot in a matter of days on a shoestring, *The Birth of a Nation* was made over a period of weeks and cost over $100,000. It featured a cast of hundreds, and the script called for over 1,500 individual camera shots.

Behind the camera was the amazing Billy Bitzer. Griffith's camera operator ran across Mathew Brady's photographs of the Civil War in a library one day. After closely studying photograph after photograph, Bitzer attempted to re-create the look of Brady's wet-collodion plates for the movie. That's why the skies have the same washed-out look in *The Birth of a Nation* as in the Brady plates. That's why there's the same great contrast between light and dark. This can even be observed in the sharp degree of difference between the uniforms worn by the soldiers of the South and the North.

During the shooting of this film, Griffith developed techniques that are commonplace in filmmaking today:

- **Close-up:** camera at close range to the subject, or in more recent films using a telescopic lens. Griffith used this technique for its psychological and dramatic effects.
- **Flashback:** film's present time interrupted in order to put in events from the past
- **Fade-in:** gradual appearance of an image
- **Fade-out:** gradual disappearance of an image

How did the public receive what was advertised as "the greatest picture ever made"? Though the price for a ticket in one New York City theater went for the unheard-of price of two dollars, *The Birth of a Nation* ran for almost a year.

More controversial by far than the ticket price was the issue of race relations as shown in the film. Oswald Garrison Villard, the grandson of the abolitionist William Lloyd Garrison, wrote in *The Nation* that the film was "a deliberate attempt to humiliate ten million American citizens and portray them as nothing but beasts." D. W. Griffith admitted that the film had been made from a Southern viewpoint, but he defended it, saying: "Of whatever excesses or outrages the blacks may be guilty, these they commit as blind and misguided, if violent, pawns of their satanic new white masters from the North."

All around the country demonstrators protested the showing of the film. In Boston alone, five thousand marched to the state capitol.

D. W. Griffith endlessly defended his film on the grounds that censorship was loose in the land. As he stated before the Virginia legislature in 1920:

The right of free speech has cost centuries upon centuries of untold suffering and agonies; it has cost rivers of blood.... The motion picture is a medium of expression as clean and decent as any mankind has ever discovered. A people that would allow the suppression of this form of speech would unquestionably submit to the suppression of that which we all consider so highly, the printing press.

The controversy over the film has continued. Until 1952, the film was still banned in Baltimore.

Unlike *The Great Train Robbery* that had been made in New Jersey, *The Birth of a Nation* had been filmed in California. Why were more and more movie companies moving from the East Coast to the West Coast? The light was more dependable in California, and there were fewer cloudy days when filming had to be postponed.

As more and more motion pictures were made, there was a growing pressure to control the content. George Eastman opposed this pressure.

"The censorship of motion pictures demanded in some directions is all wrong," Eastman declared in 1922. "If the product emanating [coming forth] from the producing studios needs reformation [a change for the better], that reformation should be accomplished at the source, not by subsequent mutilation [removal of important scenes] of the film or by damming the flow of the industry."

After several studies showed how movies could increase student learning and understanding, Eastman started an educational film division. But there was no one who spoke more glowingly of the promise of movies in the classroom than Thomas Edison did in 1925. "I should say that in ten years," predicted Edison, "textbooks as the principal medium of teaching will be as obsolete as the horse and carriage are now."

One of the next great advances in motion pictures was the rise of the talkies. In the mid-1920s, Western Electric and Bell Laboratories had developed a film sound track (a narrow magnetic strip along one edge of motion picture film that carried the sound recording), but no studios showed any interest. Then Warner Brothers, on the brink of bankruptcy, gambled $800,000 on the invention and in 1927 turned out *The Jazz Singer*. It was a roaring success. Overnight, the movie industry changed. Silent movies became as extinct as dinosaurs.

The Jazz Singer starred Al Jolson. The movie studios had already started the star system. Audiences fell for movie stars in a big way, often seeming more interested in their personal lives than in their acting on the screen. This tendency continues to this day.

The camera that Billy Bitzer had used for D. W. Griffith was a hand-cranked Pathé model from France. George Eastman wanted to put a better movie camera into the hands of everyone who wanted to film a family's own major events, such as the first steps of a baby, a first birthday party, the first day of school. The idea was that the Kodak movie camera would be small, lightweight, and easy to use, just as the original Kodak had been. In fact, this camera's home movies would be motion picture's version of the snapshot.

In 1914, F. W. Barnes of the Hawk-Eye Works showed Eastman the movie camera he had come up with for home use. The camera itself served as a projector when the back was taken off and replaced by a projection lamp. Eastman liked the idea, but the film presented a problem. Barnes's system did not use safety film, which was something that Eastman insisted upon for home use. Also, the two-step film processing—developing the exposed strip and printing on another strip—was too complicated.

John Capstaff, an English scientist who had recently joined Eastman Kodak in Rochester, studied Barnes's film-processing problem. He changed the film processing from positive-negative to a film reversal. Reversing the exposed film from a negative to a positive may have saved on film, but it called for the camera operator to expose the film perfectly every time. Otherwise, it would be too overexposed, and there would not be enough contrast between the light and dark areas of the film. Or the film would be too underexposed, and the images would be so dark and dense it would be difficult to tell what was going on. Capstaff and Eastman knew it was not realistic to expect the average film operator to be able to expose the film perfectly.

The Hawk-Eye Works was given the go-ahead to design a home movie camera, and in 1920, completed a model of the first Cine-Kodak. (Pronounced sin-EE, *cine* is an abbreviation of the word *cinema* and means "motion picture.") Sixteen was a significant number for this camera. The film was shot at 16 frames per second, and the film width was 16 millimeters. (The 16mm film included 10mm for the image and 3mm on each side for the sprocket holes.)

One of the most difficult things about using the Cine-

Kodak was getting used to cranking the camera at the correct speed of two cranks every second. Eastman wanted to show that the average person could load and operate the camera. At that time Eastman had Harold Gleason, an organist, play classical music for him every morning. The wife of Eastman's organist was asked to film her son's birthday party. Marion Gleason admitted that she had been terrified, but the results encouraged Eastman to begin the development of another complete photographic system.

Ready in 1923, the Cine-Kodak home movie system was expensive. The camera and tripod, projector and screen sold for over $300; and each two-minute film cost over $3. But it was now as simple to use as the original Kodak had been. "You press the button, we do the rest."

The Cine-Kodak also represented a giant step forward for photography. Moving from still photos to movies could be viewed as being as significant an advance as when Eastman originally went from dry plates to film.

George Eastman and friends around a campfire during one of his camping trips.

As busy as work had been at Kodak Park, Eastman was beginning to enjoy getting away from Rochester. From the time Eastman turned fifty, he had been going on camping trips. Many of these camping trips could hardly have been considered roughing it. On one outing there had been *forty* pack animals to carry the various tents and trunks of supplies, including a vast collection of cooking equipment, an area that Eastman took personal charge of.

In 1926, George Eastman went on an African safari with the documentary filmmakers Martin and Osa Johnson. A safari, even for Eastman, represented the ultimate camping trip.

One afternoon in Africa, Eastman was shooting a movie with his Cine-Kodak. Spotting a rhinoceros some distance away, Eastman started walking toward it. Osa Johnson recalled that moment as if it had been frozen in time.

"We had no way of knowing," said Osa Johnson, "what Mr. Eastman would do under the circumstances and were completely unprepared when he started toward the animal, taking pictures with his little camera as he went."

"Suddenly, the big beast decided to resent Mr. Eastman, snorted, lowered his head, and charged. Never have I seen a greater exhibition of coolness than Mr. Eastman now displayed," recalled Mrs. Johnson. "Instead of turning and running, which anyone else would have done, he stood quietly, still facing the animal, and when, snorting and ferocious, it was within perhaps fifteen feet of him, he simply sidestepped it, like a toreador, and actually touched its side as it passed."

The Cine-Kodak had already stood up to many technical problems and had now stood up to a charging rhinoceros as well.

In July 1928, Eastman invited a few of his friends and fellow scientists to witness the wonder of *color* home movies. During the day, a Cine-Kodak was used to film the guests. That evening the results were shown.

"I should consider it must be the greatest development in photography," marveled General John J. Pershing, the commander of the U.S. forces during World War I, and one of the guests.

C. E. K. Mees, the scientist who had spearheaded "the English invasion" of Rochester in 1912 and was, in Eastman's words, "the highest authority on color photography in the world," offered this explanation to the awestruck guests:

> When the trigger of the camera is pressed, light reflected from the subject passes selectively through the three-color filter, on through the camera lens, and thence through the tiny embossed lenses on the film to the sensitive emulsion coating on the opposite side, where it is recorded.... In order to project the pictures, the developed film is put in the projector which contains exactly the same optical system reversed.

"It is entirely simple," sighed another guest, the thoroughly impressed Thomas Alva Edison. "I worked on it myself several years ago, but I made a failure of it. Anybody can use it now."

A New Role for Photography

The film made by the Eastman Kodak Company had come a long way since the days of American Film. Just how far was shown after the tragic expedition to the South Pole in 1912 of the English explorer Captain Robert Scott. After reaching the South Pole, Captain Scott returned to the last camp, carrying the films of the expedition. During a nine-day blizzard, Scott and two of his companions lost their lives. In the ice and snow alongside their frozen bodies was hidden the record of their trip.

"These films lay beside their dead bodies for eight months before the search party, on account of the months of darkness, were able to reach the spot," explained H. G. Ponting, the official photographer for Scott's expedition.

They were then discovered and brought back to the winter quarters hut, where they were developed in January, 1913. The films have therefore passed through the tropics, through one Antarctic winter buried in the snow, and have lain through another winter in the temperature which must have fallen 80 degrees below zero, before development and after exposure; and they were two and one half years old. I have these negatives now and enclose a print from one of them. They must beyond all question be the most remarkable negatives in the world. Without them we should never have actually seen how Captain Scott and his companions looked when at the uttermost extremity of the earth nor what they found there, the tent of the Norwegian Amundsen, who reached this goal just a month earlier.

The difficult conditions that this film had undergone were more extreme than any test it might have undergone in the laboratory. The results, in a word, were spectacular.

Another great advance for film would be to make the leap from black and white to color. For several years, there had been two theories about how to produce color film.

One was the additive theory. This theory stated that by adding the three primary colors of red, yellow, and blue in varying combinations, all the colors found in nature can be reproduced.

The other was the subtractive theory. This theory was based on a very different idea. By subtracting, or taking away, the unwanted colors from white light, the desired shades of color can be achieved.

In 1904, Joseph Thacher Clarke, Eastman's roving troubleshooter, thought that by using the additive theory he had solved the riddle of making color photographs. His solution at first seemed simple enough. It was to take three successive photographs using three different color filters. Within the walls of the laboratory, it worked well enough. In the outside world, however, it proved to be totally impractical.

"If we could achieve a practical color process," speculated George Eastman, "it might have quite a vogue."

In 1912, Eastman visited Wratten & Wainwright, an English dry-plate company. Eastman was so impressed with one of the company's scientists, Charles Edward Kenneth Mees, that he ended up buying the company and moving it to Rochester. Eastman's plans were to set up a research laboratory at Kodak Park with Dr. Mees as director.

This was a wonderful opportunity for C. E. K. Mees to put his philosophy into practice, a philosophy in which Eastman also believed. "What one had to do was to add to the total of scientific knowledge," said Dr. Mees, "and when you went, as you would in the end, you could feel that you had done something in adding to that total."

In 1913, Mees opened the Research Laboratory with a staff of twenty, among them John Capstaff. The Research Laboratory split its time between developing new materials and processes and doing research on understanding basic photographic processes. Mees was careful not to promise any quick miracles.

The next time an Eastman Kodak employee seemed to be close to discovering a method for practical color photography was in 1914. Using the subtractive theory, John Capstaff took two pictures, one with a green filter and one with a red filter. After the negatives were dyed, they displayed their complementary, or contrasting, colors. The green filter produced red-orange colors. The red filter made blue-green colors. Unfortunately, though, when the two negatives were combined, the results were uneven. Although the photographs of people displayed good skin tones, the scenes of landscapes looked washed-out.

One of Eastman's primary long-range goals for the Research Laboratory was the development of a practical color process that would have commercial possibilities. By the mid-1920s, there was a Kodak transparency process called the Berthan process that used a series of lens filters. This led in 1928 to a Kodacolor process for home movies. It did not catch on right away because either very bright natural or artificial light was required. But it did change the outlook for color.

"With the coming of this new process amateur movies will be in color," Dr. Mees later wrote. "There is no longer any need for us to pretend that the world is in mono-chrome and to represent the glorious world in which we live by a gray ghost on the screen."

The same "glorious world" of color also was waiting for use in commercial motion pictures as well as in still photography, especially snapshots. The day would eventually come when color film would all but replace black-and-white film.

(It wasn't until 1935—three years after Eastman's death—that Kodak introduced Kodacolor. Kodacolor used multilayered film: the first layer was sensitive to blue light, the second layer to green, and the third to red. After exposure, each layer is developed separately by what are called coupler developers.)

The research facilities that had developed color photography had also been turned toward the war effort. Although World War I began in 1914, the lengthening shadows of the conflict did not fall on the United States

93

until later. But in April 1917, the United States officially entered World War I.

Soon afterward, George Eastman offered to provide the facilities for a school, as well as qualified instructors and all the necessary equipment, for training the military in aerial photography. (The first aerial photograph had been taken from a balloon by Nadar in 1858.) Eastman was not looking to make a profit. His goal was to help the Allies.

The government, however, turned down the offer. The reason given was that it wanted to keep all the instruction at the military bases. Eastman wondered if the real reason wasn't that the government didn't want to accept any favors from one of the so-called trusts.

Nevertheless, Eastman continued his interest in aerial photography by having his company develop a special camera for use on airplane flights. Nicknamed "Whistling Jim," this camera would be able to take fifty photographs rapidly—each photograph six inches square and on film.

Film had not been used before in aerial photography because details did not show up as clearly as they did on glass plates. A crew in Rochester was working overtime perfecting a special emulsion to make film more sensitive.

On its first test flight, the pilot pushed a lever to start the camera. Then the pilot continued to fly over the area around Buffalo. After the plane had landed, the film was developed and examined. The surrounding countryside had been captured in crisp, clear detail. There was one drawback, however. If the camera had to be reloaded in midair, someone other than the pilot, perhaps the navigator, would have to do it.

Why was the camera considered to be so important in

the war effort? The reason was spotlighted in an article in *Scientific American* on November 24, 1917: "That peaceful-looking camera, which we use on Sundays for snapping pictures of our friends and of pretty views, becomes a deadly instrument when it is brought into the military world.... Why the camera should be so deadly in the war zone is due to the ease with which any object can be accurately described by means of a photograph."

Specialists in aerial photography would be able to detect, in photographs taken from altitudes as high as 20,000 feet, the movement of trucks, tanks, and troops, and even to locate new trenches as they were being dug. Commanders in the field would be able to base their battle plans on this invaluable, detailed information on the enemy's strengths and weaknesses.

In addition to aerial photography, the U.S. government was also interested in Kodak's cellulose acetate. Would it be used for movies? As a matter of fact, Eastman did think it was important for the troops to have movies available. "I believe that supplying the camps with motion pictures is a highly important feature in maintaining the morale of the troops," he wrote.

More than motion pictures, though, the government needed cellulose acetate in order to cover the fabric wings of airplanes. This would enable planes to fly even during the worst weather.

A major part of George Eastman's war effort was doing something he was an expert at doing, and that was raising money. Eastman seemed to have a golden touch. Time and again, Eastman would lead fund-raising drives for the War Chest (money to finance a war) and the Red Cross in the Rochester area. By the example of his own generous giving and his firm pressure on other wealthy persons, Eastman always helped Rochester to exceed its quotas.

Eastman, however, publicly recognized the small giver as the one who made a much bigger sacrifice. "In the first place, my friends," Eastman told a gathering celebrating the collection of over $4 million for the War Chest, "you all know just as well as I know that the real giver is that poor woman who took over the family washing and thereby saved an additional fifty cents a week in order that she might put it in this fund. That is the real giver."

In all, Eastman made available over $27 million in war loans and government bonds to the American and Allied governments during World War I. The Eastman Kodak Company lent another $20 million.

Seven months after the U.S. government had turned down Eastman's offer to set up a training facility to teach military personnel aerial photography, Eastman was asked to restate his offer. This time it was accepted. Immediately, Eastman provided the barracks and classroom space for soldiers, as well as the photographic equipment and the instructors for teaching how to operate cameras, process film, and interpret aerial photographs. What had once been taught at Langley Field in Virginia, Fort Sill in Oklahoma, and Cornell University was now all located in Rochester. With all the soldiers in their broad-brimmed campaign hats, leather leggings, and brown uniforms, Kodak Park had taken on the air of a military post.

Another crucial project was to develop effective camouflage for ships. In a corner of the physics department at Kodak Park a tank of water was rocked in an imitation of rough seas, tossing small model ships about on its waves. Up periscope, and a tiny submarine surveyed the scene. It was through this type of experimentation that Eastman Kodak was able to figure out a camouflage that would eventually help real ships slip past real enemy submarines.

By 1918, specialists in aerial photography were graduating each month from the school at Kodak Park. In addition, Kodak was making 3,600 pounds of cellulose acetate every day for airplanes and gas masks. Instead of cameras, the Hawk-Eye Works was making gun sights and trench periscopes. But there was still a need for lenses, tripods, aerial cameras, and film for both still photographs

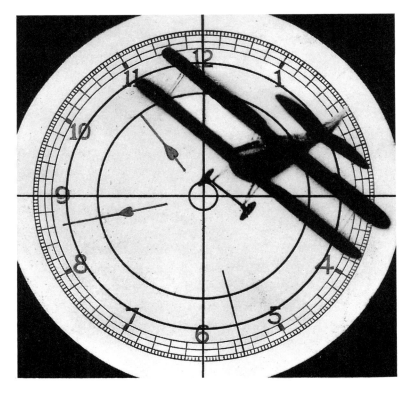

An aerial photograph taken with a World War I machine-gun camera in 1918.

and movies. Kodak was also producing X-ray film to help doctors diagnose the injuries of soldiers wounded in the horrendous bloodshed of World War I.

Finally, the "war to end war" came to a halt at eleven o'clock in the morning of November 11, 1918. One of the unexpected outcomes of the war was that under the guidance of George Eastman, the Eastman Kodak Company had become one of the leading players on the world stage. It was a far cry from the days when it was only a small dry-plate manufacturer on the third floor of a factory building in Rochester.

9

Focus on Education

Perhaps George Eastman had once needed to be treated by a dentist and had not been able to afford the treatment. Whether or not that had been the case, he knew what it was like to be caught in that situation. Eastman firmly believed that "money spent in the care of children's teeth is one of the wisest expenditures that can be made."

Beginning in 1909, George Eastman began contributing to the Rochester Dental Society. Then in 1914 he heard wonderful things about the Forsyth Infirmary in Boston. Eastman wanted to start something similar for the people of Rochester.

What happened next shows what a force for change Eastman could be. He told the city officials that if there was enough support for the project, he would provide whatever else was needed. Eastman approached outside projects with the same determination and imagination that he brought to the workings of Kodak.

The city of Rochester would have to raise $10,000 a year for five years. It would also have to hire enough staff to examine and clean the teeth of all the city's schoolchildren twice each year. If the city displayed that kind of support, then Eastman could be counted on to give $30,000 to build a hospital, $750,000 to endow the project, and $40,000 a year operating expenses for the first five years. (An endowment is money or property donated to provide a permanent income for an institution. An endowment of $750,000 back then would equal one of almost $8 million in 1992.)

In 1917, only three years after Eastman had first heard about the dental clinic in Boston, the Rochester Dispensary officially opened its doors to the people of Rochester. In 1919, this clinic, which Eastman founded, treated some 48,000 people. About 42,000 of them had been able to pay only the minimum fee of five cents.

"I have been so much interested lately in medical affairs," remarked Eastman, "that I almost feel like a doctor myself these days."

But Eastman did not stop there. He went on to establish dental clinics in all the cities of Europe where there were Eastman Kodak plants. This meant that George Eastman would be helping people, especially children, in the following capital cities: London, England; Paris, France; Rome, Italy; Stockholm, Sweden; and Brussels, Belgium.

The importance that George Eastman placed on supporting education that he had first displayed in 1887 (when he gave fifty dollars to help a local trade school) was most dramatically shown by his long association with the Massachusetts Institute of Technology (MIT), just outside of Boston.

Frank W. Lovejoy, who was to become one of George

Eastman's most valuable employees, had gone to the Massachusetts Institute of Technology. So had Henry Reichenbach and Darragh de Lancey. Over the years Eastman was to get so many of his outstanding people, especially chemists, from MIT that a special relationship was formed between this institution in Cambridge, Massachusetts, and this businessman from Rochester, New York.

In 1912, Eastman asked Lovejoy to arrange a meeting for him with the president of MIT, Dr. Richard C. Maclaurin. In terms of the future of MIT, it couldn't have come at a better time. Dr. Maclaurin had high hopes for buying fifty acres of land along the banks of the Charles River and starting a major building program.

"At this meeting, as at many others since," observed the president of MIT about George Eastman,

> I could not fail to be impressed with his capacity to go to the heart of a problem quickly and see immediately what the main points are and to keep to those points in later discussion. He was interested in Technology's problems, but made it clear that his continued interest would depend upon its problems being tackled in a bold way and in a liberal spirit.... He likes things done well, but does not think they are well done unless they are done economically.

In this description of the businessman from Rochester in action, Richard C. Maclaurin went to the heart of what made George Eastman the success that he was.

Eastman thought over the points brought up during the meeting and quickly decided that he wanted to help. He immediately presented a gift of two and a half million dollars to the building fund. One of the requirements that

Eastman made was that matching funds must be raised. Another requirement was that his real name must not be used. Instead, Eastman wanted to be known simply as "Mr. Smith."

Over the years, "Mr. Smith" gave more and more gifts to MIT. The students even made up a song to pay tribute to their legendary anonymous donor:

Hurrah! Hurrah! for Tech and Boston beans,
    Hurrah! Hurrah! for "Smith," whoe'er that means;
May he always have a hundred million in his jeans,
    So we'll get—what we want—when we want it.

By 1919, Eastman had given the school some $11 million. From its modest beginnings in 1861—fifteen students were enrolled by 1865—the Massachusetts Institute of Technology now had the land and the buildings and would soon have the endowment to become one of the premier engineering schools in the world.

When "Mr. Smith" presented MIT with Kodak stock as an endowment in 1920, the name of the benefactor (one who gives help or financial aid) was finally out of the bag. It was obvious whose name was on the stock certificates. The national guessing game over the true identity of "Mr. Smith" could now come to an end.

"The only reason I ever had for withholding my name from connection with my original gifts to the Institute," explained George Eastman, "was to avoid the nuisance of the notoriety of big giving."

The appreciation of George Eastman's extraordinary gifts began to pour in. One letter of thanks was from a trustee at MIT, A. Lawrence Lowell: "I do not know that any man in the world has done so much to help an institution of engineering as you have done for this."

Eastman's generosity toward schools did not stop with MIT. He also believed that education was the key for assisting African Americans in achieving equality in the United States. That lay behind his financial support of two leading schools for African Americans, the Tuskegee Normal and Industrial Institute (now Tuskegee University) and the Hampton Normal and Agricultural Institute (now Hampton University).

The Tuskegee Normal and Industrial Institute had been the dream of Booker T. Washington, who as the first president of the school, had opened its doors in 1881. In 1903, Andrew Carnegie gave $600,000 for a library; by 1909, there was a 15,000-book library. Including the surrounding farmland and timberland, the school located in Tuskegee, Alabama, was spread out over 2,000 acres. The 200-acre campus featured a hundred buildings—all designed and built by the faculty and students.

To feel proud about the priority he had given to the role of education, Eastman needed to look no further than two of the prominent African Americans at the Tuskegee Institute. Booker T. Washington was a world-famous educator, and George Washington Carver was a world-famous agricultural chemist and botanist.

The Hampton Normal and Agricultural Institute had been opened in 1868 in Hampton, Virginia. One of the most important early graduates was Booker T. Washington. Ten years later, the important step was taken of inviting Native Americans to join its student body.

The school combined both study and practical work experience. Many of the students worked during the day and attended the school at night. The underlying idea behind this school was that people not only would be able to learn a useful trade, but also would then be able to teach others the skills they had learned.

George Eastman could easily have identified with these working students. Working all day and studying at night was how he had eventually broken away from his job at the bank and started what had become the Eastman Kodak Company.

Eastman also liked nothing better than working with his hands. One day at his farm retreat in North Carolina, Eastman was fixing the plumbing. After watching for a while, a guest observed how happy Eastman seemed to be. "I would rather wipe a lead joint well," replied Eastman, "than anything I know of."

Another major project that Eastman started in 1920 was the establishment of a medical complex at the University of Rochester that would some day rival that of the Johns Hopkins University in Baltimore, Maryland. It included schools of medicine, surgery, and dentistry, with the school of dentistry working closely with the Rochester Dispensary.

Eastman also established a hospital, the Henry A. Strong Memorial Hospital, to go with the medical complex. He named it in honor of his old friend, partner, and first president of the company, Colonel Strong, who had died in 1919 at the age of eighty-one.

Another friend had once asked Eastman why he gave so much money to schools. "The answer was easy," recalled Eastman. "In the first place, the progress of the world depends almost entirely upon education.

"Fortunately, the most permanent institutions of man are educational," continued Eastman. "They usually endure even when governments fall; hence the selection of educational institutions."

"The reason that I selected a limited number of institutions," explained Eastman, "was because I wanted to cover certain kinds of education, and felt that I could get results with [these] institutions...quicker and more directly than if the money was spread."

Eastman displayed the businesslike approach toward education that he had brought to everything else in his life. "Under the best conditions it takes considerable time, sometimes years, to develop the wise expenditure of money in any line, no matter how well prepared one may be."

Nevertheless, creeping more and more into his thinking was an acknowledgment of his own mortality. "I am now upwards of seventy years old, and feel that I would like to see results from this money within the natural term of my remaining years," Eastman wrote.

To help fund projects at the University of Rochester, including a College for Women, Eastman gave away much of his fortune. On one day alone in 1924 he signed over $30 million. "One of the reasons why I wish this disposition of my Kodak stock," acknowledged Eastman, "is that it separates me from making money for myself and will give me the benefit of a somewhat more detached position in respect to human affairs. I look forward with interest to finding out how much the changed conditions will affect my outlook on current affairs."

George Eastman may have given away most of his money, but he never regarded money as evil. He felt that his money could be employed for the common good. Instead of simply getting rid of his money, Eastman spent a great deal of time and effort in exploring the best way to donate it. He searched out positive ways for his money to help make people's lives better.

Eastman employed his money to help all aspects of people's lives. He gave money to educate people's minds to help them get better jobs. He gave money to improve and repair their bodies. And he gave money to make their leisure time more profitable. George Eastman's money went to improve the entire human being.

Eastman also was able to see a lighter side to his giving. "It is more fun to give money than to will it," he confessed. "And that is why I give."

Then Eastman went on to explain his philosophy in more detail: "If a man has wealth, he has to make a choice, because there is the money heaping up. He can keep it together in a bunch and then leave it for others to administer after he is dead. Or, he can get it into action and have fun, while he is still alive."

Ever the cold-eyed realist, Eastman added, "I prefer getting it into action and adapting it to human needs, and making the plan work."

Eastman's money was usually presented to an entire institution. In one case, however, it was to endow a single chair (position of authority) at a university. In 1929, Eastman gave a $200,000 endowment for a George Eastman Visiting Professorship at Oxford University in England. The purpose was "the promotion of knowledge and understanding between all who speak the English language."

Eastman had always felt close to the English. (The Eastmans and Kilbourns had moved from England to America in the seventeenth century.) This feeling had only been strengthened by the so-called "English invasion" in 1912. That was when C. E. K. Mees, John Capstaff, and others journeyed from England to Rochester to begin the Research Laboratory.

In addition to Eastman's belief that "the progress of the world depends almost entirely on education," it may also have been that Eastman learned the true value of an education the hard way. Having been a public school dropout himself, Eastman had never known the experience of going to high school. He had not enjoyed the privilege of attending college or pursuing a particular course of interest in graduate school.

"The man I knew best," said Frank W. Lovejoy, the fourth president of the Eastman Kodak Company,

> of all the men who were unable to get a college education was George Eastman. He left school at thirteen or so, as he had to support his widowed mother. Mr. Eastman valued higher educational training highly—as evidenced by his magnificent gifts to the Massachusetts Institute of Technology, the University of Rochester, and other institutions here and elsewhere. He was a truly cultured man and, of course, wholly self-educated.

10

Time-out for Music

Woonan hen George Eastman was sixteen years old, he put money down to buy a flute on the installment plan. Although he was to take lessons over the next two years, he never displayed much musicality. As a matter of fact, George failed even to master "Annie Laurie," a song that he practiced over and over.

Colonel Henry Alvah Strong never seemed to tire in telling one story in particular about his partner: After all those music lessons, upon hearing "Annie Laurie" played correctly years later, George Eastman didn't even recognize the song.

A lack of musical talent, however, did not mean that George Eastman did not possess a deep appreciation and love for music. Indeed, few people anywhere have done as much to bring the joy of music to others.

"When I was a young man," recalled Eastman, "I worked at a ledger eleven hours a day; by no magic could a performance such as that be made alluring. It was sheer work, unpleasant, but inescapable in civilization. This situation, I find, confronts a very large part of the population."

The problem, as Eastman saw it, was not with work. "I am not at all of the opinion that people have been ground down by industry," explained Eastman. "I do not think that we have ever created enough outside interests. Leisure is unfruitful because it is not used productively."

Because "work, a very great deal of work, is drudgery," Eastman continued, it is necessary to improve leisure time. First of all, leisure is not idle time; it is not wasting time. "It is necessary for people to have an interest in life outside of an occupation."

"What you do in your working hours determines what you have," believed Eastman. "What you do in your leisure hours determines what you are."

Eastman believed that one of the major ways to make leisure time productive was through music. Although he may not have displayed any musical talent, he certainly did appreciate music. It appeared that Eastman received the same enormous pleasure from music that William Congreve, an English dramatist, described in his 1697 play, *The Mourning Bride*:

> Music has charms to soothe a savage breast,
> To soften rocks, or bend a knotted oak.

Not by any means, though, was Eastman's love of music something he kept personal or private. He had an overwhelming desire to share his love of music with others by making music available to everyone.

One of Eastman's goals was to make Rochester a music capital. Also, behind a great deal of Eastman's thinking was how best to go about educating the public to appreciate music.

"It is fairly easy to employ skillful musicians. It is impossible to buy an appreciation of music," explained Eastman. "Yet, without appreciation, without the presence of a large body of people who understand music and who get joy out of it, any attempt to develop the musical resources of any city is doomed to failure."

In 1918, Eastman gave the University of Rochester the funds to buy the Institute of Musical Art. The next year he began the building program of the Eastman School of Music.

In 1922, a beautiful theater with state-of-the-art acoustics (the science of sound in an auditorium) that could seat over three thousand people was built. At first, Eastman wanted to name this theater the Academy of Music, but he eventually accepted a committee's decision that it should be called the Eastman Theater.

It occurred to Eastman that a special use existed for the Eastman Theater. He realized that it would be a good idea to use the large theater to show motion pictures accompanied by a symphony orchestra. That way, the people who enjoyed movies would learn to appreciate the time-honored beauties of music. Similarly, the people who appreciated music would learn to enjoy the newfangled art of the moving picture show.

Although the film image was to be combined with music, the key to Eastman's plans was an orchestra. Eastman believed that "an orchestra can be made a big factor in education." He was the leader in a movement to begin a full-time orchestra for the city of Rochester.

Eastman was quick to realize, though, that during the whole concert season a potential audience of only 150,000 people would be able to attend. However, if these symphony concerts could be broadcast over the radio at the same time, then ten times that number of people would be able to enjoy this music. "[T]he ears of the populace will be so educated that they will demand good music and be satisfied with nothing else," Eastman wrote.

In addition to the music school, there was another building project that Eastman had been very proud of. After living with his mother for many years in the house that he had bought in 1890, Eastman had a thirty-seven-room mansion built in 1905 at 900 East Avenue. It was a home of great craftsmanship and luxury: twelve bathrooms and nine fireplaces. The same attention to detail George Eastman displayed in business, he applied to his everyday life as well. On the grounds was even a greenhouse for raising the flowers that his mother loved.

What did all of this extravagance signal? Yes, it was the age of mansions, many of which can be visited today. Moreover, it may have been that George Eastman was paying back Maria Eastman for all those years of struggle, as well as for believing in him. And, of course, there was no need to take in lodgers to pay for it all.

Eastman's approach and typical thoroughness were even evident in his collection of art. Eastman loved painting, but he bought what he liked and what looked right with the decor, or furnishings, of the various rooms at 900 East Avenue. This meant that he never bought art until he had at first lived with it.

Once, Eastman had a painting out on loan from an art dealer. Eastman liked it well enough, but he felt it didn't fit in with the rest of his art collection. It just didn't go with the paintings by Corot, Van Dyke, Gainsborough, Hals, Homer, Millet, and Rembrandt. When the art dealer became upset and pressured Eastman to buy the painting, Eastman quickly and quietly spoke his mind: "The only thing I can do is to assure you that you will probably never have occasion to be disappointed again in any transaction with me."

With the mansion completed, Eastman threw a New Year's Eve party. Throughout the house, vases overflowed with flowers from the greenhouse. White-gloved waiters carrying silver trays glided among the 1,200 guests. At the appointed hour, a small orchestra began to play. It was a dance, but Eastman did not like to dance. There was even a quartet to sing a medley, and among the songs was "Annie Laurie." In the years to come, there would be many, many parties at the Eastman mansion, but no more dances.

George Eastman knew people from many different walks of life. His acquaintances were as varied as his interests. And Eastman seemed to be interested in just about everything. Whether it was a painting or an oriental rug, a rare strain of roses or the landscaping of a park, a new camp stove or an experienced string quartet, Eastman often knew about it and wanted to know more.

For a quarter of a century, a mainstay in the life of Rochester society was Sunday night dinner at the Eastman house. This was a comfortable but very gracious evening filled with good talk, good food, and good music. (Until her death in 1907, George's mother, Maria Kilbourn Eastman, often served as hostess.)

George Eastman was in the habit of greeting all his guests one by one, and it was not unheard of for there to be as many as a hundred people at dinner. In fact, Eastman rarely ate alone, no matter what day of the week or what meal of the day it was. The dinner guests were free to wander through the book-lined study, the plant-filled conservatory, even up to the third floor where there were trophies from George's camping trips in the United States and Canada. Or the guests could walk past the majestic elephant head on the main floor and out to the terraces and formal gardens.

Dinner could be an elaborate affair with many courses or as simple as Boston baked beans. But no matter what it was, after dinner there was always classical music. Often, the music would be provided by a string quartet. A hush would fall over the guests as the four musicians—a first and second violin, a cello, and a viola (halfway in size and sound between a violin and a cello)—sat on the edges of their chairs, ready to strike the first note.

With its mathematical precision and daredevil artistry, the string quartet would appeal to Eastman's sense of order and risk taking within set boundaries. Wearing his typical quizzical expression (one corner of his mouth appearing to turn up slightly, the other corner down), George would take it all in, studying the musicians through his round, gold-framed glasses, tapping his toe, not missing a beat.

George Eastman showed his belief in the soothing powers of music by his generosity in all matters musical. But above all, he was a practical person. Because Eastman found that music put him in the proper frame of mind for the day's activities, he not only had an organ installed in his house, but he also hired an organist. Every morning at seven-thirty, Mr. Gleason dropped by to play. However, it wasn't as if Eastman liked all classical music. Eastman requested that Gleason play anything, as long as it wasn't Bach. His favorite was Wagner.

"Do not imagine that I am a reformer—far from that," said Eastman.

It is simply I am interested in music personally, and I am led thereby, merely to want to share my pleasure with others.

What I am personally interested in, and have been from the start, is the making of Rochester a truly musical city. By that I mean where the inhabitants love to listen to good music. Everything else to my mind is secondary to this, but in order to accomplish it we must have a music school here and one of the desirable connections is a fine orchestra.

By 1924, the school of music was in full operation. In addition to the Eastman Theater for concerts, there were studios, classrooms, a music library and a regular library, Kilbourn Hall (named for his mother) for chamber music recitals, and dormitories.

In almost no time at all the Eastman School of Music had enrolled two thousand students, its capacity. Students even had to be turned away. "Fond parents are often anxious to have children with no musical capabilities taught in the Eastman School," noted Eastman regretfully, "and it is sometimes very difficult to satisfy them when they have to be rejected."

Building and staffing a music school had not been an easy task. "But it has all been very interesting and nothing to lose any sleep over, and plenty to laugh at," commented Eastman. "I am learning a lot about psychology."

Although it benefited many, the Eastman School of Music did not reach the population at large. So, Eastman again set about to ensure that Rochester would become a music capital by having a fine symphony orchestra. In addition to their regular concerts, the Rochester Symphony Orchestra performed as many as sixty concerts in the city high schools. These concerts were free to music students on Wednesday afternoons and cost only a quarter on Sundays. To this day, the Rochester Symphony Orchestra continues to be one of the leading orchestras in the world.

Looking back over his involvement with music, especially with the University of Rochester's Eastman School of Music, George Eastman seemed both amazed and amused. He wrote: "It has given me more fun in my old age than anything I have ever tackled. When you think of it, it's a joke that one who is totally devoid of musical ability is trying to steer one of the largest musical enterprises ever proposed."

11

Fading Out

From the top of the sixteen-story office building known as the Kodak Building, George Eastman could gaze down at the intersection of Main and State streets. That was the area where George's father had started the Eastman Commercial College and George himself had begun his working life as a messenger for an insurance company. Barely a block away was the Rochester Savings Bank where George had been a bookkeeper.

Near the Kodak Building, next to where the Eastman Dry Plate Company factory had been, stood Frank Brownell's Camera Works. Across the river was the Hawk-Eye Works. And a short three miles away loomed Kodak Park. Sprawled over four hundred acres, Kodak Park contained building after specialized building for producing film, for making photographic papers, for conducting research.

The Eastman Kodak Company was a wonderful accomplishment and a gigantic success. "An organization cannot be sound unless its spirit is," explained a reflective George Eastman. "That is the lesson the man on top must learn. He must be a man of vision and progress who can understand that one can muddle along on a basis in which the human factor takes no part, but eventually there comes a fall."

Many of the day-to-day operations George Eastman eventually turned over to Frank Lovejoy. Though George wanted "to fade out of the picture," he was still at the office more often than he would have liked.

"I am trying to fix it so that I will have to come down to business only about every second rainy Thursday," joked a tongue-in-cheek Eastman, "but so many new things are continually coming up that my plan has not so far brought about the desired result. Hope springs eternal, however, and that is what keeps me going."

At long last George Eastman was to get his wish. Albert K. Chapman, whose office was nearby, recalled what those days were like: "Then there came the time when he was in his office less and less frequently. It came to be news when he was there. The word would go round—Mr. Eastman is in today. Somehow or other that made it a better day for all of us. Finally he came no more."

Eastman had once stated: "We never reach the end of anything. . . . The man who thinks he has done everything he can do has merely stopped thinking. He is what might be called 'up and out.' And, excepting that he has more money, his case really is not very different from that of the man who is 'down and out.'"

On a drive across Rochester, George Eastman could pass many of his monuments. These were not statues.

Rather they were living memorials to Eastman's success and vision.

All around Rochester stood building after building filled with learning and medicine and dentistry and music. There was the College of Arts and Science, the Medical School, and the College for Women—all at the University of Rochester. There was the Strong Memorial Hospital and the Rochester Dental Dispensary. There was the Eastman School of Music, Kilbourn Hall, the Eastman Theater. The major purpose of these different institutions was to help people lead healthier, more enjoyable lives.

Eastman had helped make Rochester a more livable city. In addition, like London before it, Rochester had become the photographic capital of the world.

By no means, however, did George Eastman restrict his gifts to Rochester. To celebrate the fiftieth anniversary of the Eastman Kodak Company, 500,000 Brownies were given away to the children in the United States. The rule was that anyone twelve years of age could pick up his or her Brownie and a roll of film after May 1, 1930. A couple of days later, every single one had been claimed.

Sometimes it seems that everything Eastman did was a good idea and turned out well. There was, though, an occasional dead end. Consider one of the causes that he championed later in life.

In 1924, Eastman came in contact with an English reformer, Moses B. Cotsworth, who was in favor of establishing a new calendar. This calendar featured thirteen months, and each month was to be divided into twenty-eight days. The reason that Eastman promoted the adoption of this new calendar was that he believed it would make doing business easier. "There is no doubt in my mind of ultimate success," predicted Eastman in 1928, "because the world moves inevitably toward the practical." Whether it does or not, the project in time disappeared from sight.

Toward the end of his life in particular, George Eastman displayed remarkable generosity toward the public. By that time he had given away $100 million, practically his entire fortune. It was as if he subscribed to the philosophy of another very rich man, Andrew Carnegie. "The man who dies rich," said Carnegie, a person who made his great fortune in steel, "dies disgraced."

George Eastman had now advanced to a higher level of richness. He had progressed beyond even taking money into consideration in the way that most human beings have to as they move through their lives. "For some time past,"

George Eastman (left) and Thomas A. Edison demonstrate the use of home-movie Kodacolor film introduced and publicized at this 1928 party at Eastman's mansion.

explained Eastman, "the accumulation of money personally has lost its importance to me."

Eastman had no sons and daughters to leave his fortune to. But then, he may not have wanted to anyway. Like Andrew Carnegie, George Eastman held in high regard the value of hard work.

Once, when a nephew tried to borrow money, Eastman had been extremely annoyed. (Carnegie once said that he was not in the practice of giving money to his relatives because it did them a great disservice.) "It seems to me, therefore, that if you need more than your father can give you," Eastman had said to his nephew, "it is up to you to go out and earn it."

In 1929, on George Eastman's seventy-fifth birthday, the *New York Times* made the following point:

> If every one who got pleasure from a snapshot or a movie film were to express gratitude to the man who initially made it possible, George Eastman would be the most bethanked man in the world.... The films that his factories produce each year would, it is estimated, reach ten times around the globe, and there is not a corner of the earth which has not been exposed to them, or to which they have not carried fleeting or treasured images.

It was sometime during 1931 that the seventy-six-year-old Eastman became worried about a spinal ailment that had the potential of causing paralysis. Eastman had once had a good friend, Walter Hubbell, whose health had failed badly in his final years. Eastman did not want anything like that to happen to him.

On March 14, 1932, George Eastman invited a few

people over to 900 East Avenue to carry out and witness an updating of his will. After the signing, he thanked everyone and shook hands. Then he excused himself and walked slowly up the stairs.

Eastman had once said about a friend's death: "One could not wish for anything better than to keep up one's interest in fishing to the age of eighty-three and then die *en route* to the river." It was as if Eastman, too, desired to die in midstream. A man with his waders on, in the cold light of morning.

It was Alice Whitney Hutchison, his personal secretary of more than forty years, who heard the pistol shot. She rushed in and found Eastman's body. Nearby, there was the following short note:

> To my friends:
> My work is done. Why wait?
> G.E.

Readers of *Variety* that week, the newspaper for people in the entertainment industry who owed so much to Eastman's vision and inventions, ran across this obituary:

"George Eastman, 77, who founded the Eastman Kodak Co., died suddenly March 14 by his own hand at his home in Rochester, N.Y., from which the Eastman interests are operated. His suicide by shooting is believed to have been caused by failing heatlh."

A friend of Eastman's, Lewis Jones, offered this explanation: "To those who know the orderly working of his mind, his passion for being useful ... his dread of an illness that might make him mentally as well as physically inactive, his act can be understood. A great man, at the end of the chapter he wrote his own finis [conclusion]."

Even so, it is sometimes hard to understand how a person who had accomplished so much and perhaps could accomplish more, a person who had been so full of ideas and full of life, could have killed himself.

The *Rochester Democrat and Chronicle* in its obituary assessed the personal qualities that had helped George Eastman achieve greatness:

[I]t was the rare combination of love for art and culture and practical, hard-headed business sense that most distinguished him. The one guided him to his business success; the artistic side of his nature showed itself in his love for beautiful surroundings, for flowers, for music, for all the finer things of life. His artistic instincts led him into photographic research in the first place; his business ability made it the foundation of a great industry.

George Eastman was a person whose many accomplishments touched millions and millions of people. Moreover, Eastman's breakthrough inventions in photography, his establishing a major part of the photographic industry, as well as his good works continue to exert their influences.

J. M. Barrie, the creator of *Peter Pan*, observed that the "life of every man is a diary in which he means to write one story, and writes another...." George Eastman's "diary," however, read far differently. Eastman seemed to have written the same story that he had meant to write: the life of an inventor, businessman, and philanthropist from Rochester.

"Eastman was a stupendous factor in the education of the modern world," declared the *New York Times* in its obituary. Among "his great gifts to the human race" were "fostering music, endowing learning and supporting science in its researches and teaching, seeking to promote health and lessen human ills, helping the poor in their struggle toward the light, making his own city the center of the arts and glorifying his own country in the eyes of the world."

CHAPTER

12

Afterimage

According to Samuel Johnson, the eighteenth-century English writer, one of the definitions of a literary classic is that its importance be still recognized a hundred years later. Perhaps the same might be said about people.

In celebration of George Eastman's hundredth birthday, the U.S. Post Office issued a George Eastman stamp. As the assistant postmaster general stated at the ceremony in Rochester on July 12, 1954:

George Eastman possessed an amazing combination of qualities, any one of which would be good reason for the issuance of this stamp. Although he was not an artist, nor a musician, nor an educator, nor a man of medicine, his name will burn brightly as a major American contributor to each of these fields of art and knowledge.

Also in honor of George Eastman's hundredth birthday, Dwight David Eisenhower, the president of the United States, added to the ever-growing stature of George Eastman by issuing the following proclamation:

> You are paying tribute to the memory of a man whose name is not only synonymous with photography but intimately connected with music, industry and philanthropy. His imagination, his diligence and courage, the breadth of his interests—these combined to give America a truly great man.

Important Dates

1854 George Eastman is born on July 12, the third of three children.

1862 Eastman's father dies suddenly. His mother rents to lodgers in an attempt to make ends meet.

1868 Eastman leaves school in order to find a job and help support the family; he works as an errand boy in an insurance company for three dollars a week.

1874 Eastman gets a job as a bookkeeper at the Rochester Savings Bank.

1877 Eastman buys photographic equipment and studies the wet-plate collodion process with George Monroe, a local photographer.

1878–79 Eastman begins to experiment with coating plates. Eventual success leads to developing and patenting his coating machine.

1880 Eastman begins to produce gelatin dry plates for sale.

1881 Eastman establishes the Eastman Dry Plate Company with the help of an investment from Colonel Henry A. Strong; Eastman quits his job at the bank to work full time in the new business.

1884 Eastman incorporates the Eastman Dry Plate & Film Company; he introduces American Film, a coated paper. Eastman and William H. Walker invent the roll holder for holding film in the camera.

1886 Eastman and Cossitt develop and abandon production of a detective camera.

1888 Eastman places his first camera on the market; he invents the word *Kodak* for this successful box camera.

1889 Eastman introduces the first commercial celluloid roll film and produces No. 1 Kodak and No. 2 Kodak cameras; the Eastman Company is incorporated.

1891 The first "Daylight" Kodak cameras are produced; Kodak Park opens.

1892 Eastman Kodak Company replaces the Eastman Company as the business's name; Eastman Kodak perfects double-coated film for motion pictures; Eastman Kodak will become major supplier of film to the motion picture industry.

1895 First Pocket Kodak becomes a popular camera that uses cartridge roll film.

1899 Eastman makes his first million dollars. He will be generous with his great wealth, giving millions to the Massachusetts Institute of Technology, the Tuskegee Normal and Industrial Institute, and the Hampton Normal and Agricultural Institute.

1900 Eastman Kodak introduces the first Brownie camera, designed by Frank Brownell. Updates of this camera remain on market for almost eighty years. Millions of people buy Brownie cameras and develop photography as a popular hobby.

1903 *The Great Train Robbery*, a film produced by Thomas Edison, displays the possibilities of motion pictures.

1904 Joseph Thacher Clarke conducts experiments for developing color film.

1911 Eastman sets up accident insurance and old-age pensions for Kodak employees.

1913 Research Laboratory opens at Kodak Park.

1914 John Capstaff experiments with color film.

1917 The United States officially enters World War I. A school of aerial photography begins at Kodak Park.

1919 The Rochester Dispensary, the dental clinic begun by Eastman, treats 48,000 people.

1923 Eastman Kodak introduces Cine-Kodak, a home movie system.

1924 The Eastman School of Music is in full operation. Eastman supports the establishment of the Rochester Symphony Orchestra.

1928 Kodacolor process is begun for home movies.

1932 George Eastman dies on March 14.

Bibliography

Ackerman, Carl W. *George Eastman.* Boston and New York: Houghton Mifflin Company, 1930.

Coe, Brian. *George Eastman and the Early Photographers.* London: Priory Press, 1973.

———. *The Birth of Photography: The Story of the Formative Years, 1800–1900.* New York: Taplinger Publishing Company, 1977.

———. *Cameras from Daguerreotypes to Instant Pictures.* London: Marshall Cavendish, 1978.

———, et al. *Techniques of the World's Great Photographers.* Oxford: Phaidon, 1981.

Collins, Douglas. *The Story of Kodak.* New York: Harry N. Abrams, 1990.

Ford, Colin, and Karl Stelnorth, eds. *You Press the Button/We Do the Rest.* London: D. Nishen, 1988.

Gernsheim, Helmut. *A Concise History of Photography*, 3rd rev. ed. New York: Dover Publications, 1986.

* Henry, Joanne Landers. *George Eastman: Young Photographer.* New York: Bobbs-Merrill, 1959.

Jenkins, Reese V. *Images and Enterprise: Technology and the American Photographic Industry, 1839 to 1925.* Baltimore and London: The Johns Hopkins University Press, 1975.

F. W. Lovejoy: The Story of a Practical Idealist. Rochester, N.Y.: The Eastman Kodak Company, 1947.

* Mitchell, Barbara. *CLICK!: A Story About George Eastman.* Minneapolis: Carolrhoda Books, 1986.

Newhall, Beaumont. *The History of Photography.* New York: The Museum of Modern Art, 1982.

————. *Latent Image: The Discovery of Photography.* Albuquerque: University of New Mexico Press, 1983.

Szarkowski, John. *Photography Until Now.* New York: The Museum of Modern Art, 1989.

Turner, Peter. *History of Photography.* New York: Exeter Books, 1987.

Williams, Richard L., ed. *Great Photographers.* Life Library of Photography. New York: Time-Life Books, 1971.

* Readers of the Pioneer in Change book *George Eastman* may find this book particularly readable.

Index

About the Author

Burnham Holmes is a writer, a teacher, and an editor. His previous books for young people are about Nefertiti, baseball, Seeing Eye dogs, a mystery, army basic training, and medicine. Most recently, he has written *The Third Amendment* and *The Fifth Amendment* for the American Heritage History of the Bill of Rights.

Holmes teaches writing at the School of Visual Arts in New York City. Burnham, Vicki, and their son, Ken, divide their time between living in New York City and near a lake in Vermont.